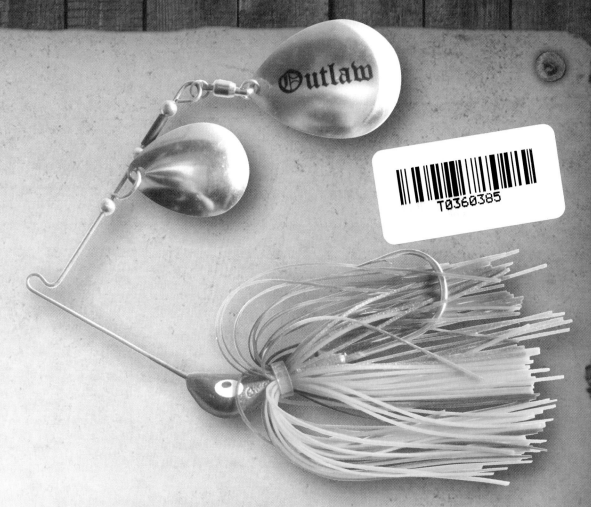

FISHING & CAMPING GUIDE TO THE
MURRAY RIVER
From Mildura to the Source

BRIAN HINSON & BILL CLASSON

Cover: Ashley Hinson with a Murray cod taken on a spinnerbait.

First Published 2008
Revised and updated 2015

Illustrations by: Trevor Hawkins

Published and distributed by
Australian Fishing Network
PO Box 544, Croydon VIC 3136
Telephone (03) 9729 8788 Faxsmile: (03) 9729 7833
Email: sales@afn.com.au
Website: www.afn.com.au

© Australian Fishing Network 2015
All right reserved

ISBN 9781 8651 3247 1

All maps in this publication are based on maps from Geoscience Australia
© Commonwealth of Australia, Geoscience Australia.

CONTENTS

Acknowledgements 4

Introduction 5

PART 1 ESSENTIAL MURRAY RIVER GUIDE LINES 6

Regulation Overview 6

Tackle Shops 8

Camping the Murray River 9

Area Map of the Murray River 12

PART 2 FISHING LOCATIONS 13

PART 3 FISHING THE MURRAY 90

The Life and Times of the Murray Cod 90

Catching a Murray Cod 92

Basic Knots 99

Other Native Fish 101

Introduced Species 106

Collecting Bait 108

Fish for the Table 112

ACKNOWLEDGEMENTS

I want to take this opportunity to publicly thank all those who gave freely of their knowledge, time and experience. It is not possible for me to list, by name, all those who have helped me, but a few people deserve special mention. I am especially grateful to the following friends: Steve Gaunt from Outlaw Spinnerbaits who accompanied me to Hume Weir and returned car to Echuca; Andrew Schulz for his descriptive directions and for being there if needed — sorry I missed you at the ramp mate; to my mate Ron Robertson for being my support crew; and to my wife, Cheryl, who gave me full support and encouragement.

BRIAN HINSON

Brian Hinson with a Murray cod caught on an Outlaw Spinnerbait.

INTRODUCTION

The Murray cod is the fish of legends. It is the subject of aboriginal folklore and has been the focus of many bushmens' yarns. There will be many fisherfolk in the Murray Darling area who have a story to tell about this ancient inhabitant of the inland waterways of Australia.

There is more, much more, to Murray cod fishing than simply hooking and hopefully landing one of these magnificent creatures. The very mention of Murray cod conjures up images of the slow green waters of the Murray River, majestic red gum forests, riverside campsites and welcoming campfires along with nature's wildlife.

Many books have been written about fish and fishing. These books may be very good but sometimes they can be very technical and aimed at experienced anglers. This can be a little daunting to an angler who only wants to know how to catch a fish. I will not assume that you already know everything there is to know about fishing or even that you know anything about fishing at all. In this book I will pass on to you, in plain language, what I have learned over 50 years of fishing for Murray cod. Although this book is about fishing for Murray cod it would not be complete without including information about the other fish you may encounter when fishing in the Murray River.

Some anglers have managed to catch a cod on their first outing but there are others who have fished for the Murray cod for a lifetime and haven't landed even one. I am aiming to help you become one of the successful anglers who can say "I caught a Murray cod".

PART 1

ESSENTIAL MURRAY RIVER GUIDE LINES

The *Pyap* at Swan Hill is one of the many paddle boats operating out of the towns along the mighty Murray River.

REGULATION OVERVIEW

BOATING REGULATIONS

The Murray River is part of New South Wales and is therefore subject to NSW Regulations.

LICENCES & REGISTRATION

In New South Wales, anyone driving a boat at 10 knots or more and 16 years of age or older must have a boat drivers licence. Visitors may use a licence issued in another Australian State or overseas if that is your usual place of residence. A restricted licence is available for people of 12 to 16 years of age. However, as these regulations are subject to change it is always best to check the website for up-to-date information.

SPEED LIMITS/RESTRICTIONS

Speed limits must be obeyed as per the signage on the waterway. You are required to comply with NSW boating laws while boating on the Murray, including carrying your licence.

For further information, check out the NSW Maritime Authority's Boating Handbook at *www.maritime.nsw.gov. au/sbh.html*

SAFETY EQUIPMENT

You must carry the safety equipment specified by NSW Maritime. This includes a Personal Flotation Device for each person on board. A bailing bucket, a fire extinguisher and a torch must be carried at all times and you are also required to have an anchor with a chain and line.

As the list of safety equipment varies with the size of the boat and the location that you are boating, a full list of item can also be found in the NSW Maritime Authority's Boating Handbook.

SUBMERGED DANGERS

Inland waterways are often murky and constantly changing so you need to be aware of possible obstructions that may be hidden below the surface. Snags are trees that have fallen and can be partly or completely submerged beneath the surface. Rock bars and sand bars can appear from seemingly nowhere, especially when the river is flowing at a very low level. Extreme care and vigilance must be taken at all times.

OTHER REGULATIONS

The following is a guide to boating regulations on the Murray River. You must refer to the relevant NSW Boating regulations to ensure all requirements are covered.

When driving a boat you should always drive on the right hand side of the river and give way to your right and always travel at a safe speed.

When boating on the Murray River it is mandatory to wear a life jacket if you are less than 12 years of age, if you are boating alone in a vessel of less than 4.8m or if the skipper judges the situation to be of heightened risk.

When water-skiing an observer in the boat is mandatory as well as the driver. The water-skier must wear a PFD (Personal Flotation Device) life jacket. When you are water-skiing you are required by law to keep 30 m clear of objects in or near the water and you must keep 60 m from a person who is in the water.

A blood alcohol content of 0.05 per cent applies to recreational vessel operators over 18 years of age. Operators under 18 years of age must have zero blood alcohol content.

For full Regulations refer to *www.maritime.nsw.gov.au/licence.html* or 131 236.

SHOOTING REGULATIONS

Firearms or Hunting are prohibited in most Murray River Parklands. Call 13 1963 for Parks Victoria and 03 5881 2266 for Forests NSW.

FISHING REGULATIONS

The Murray River and its banks are part of New South Wales. Lake Hume is designated as Victoria to the Bethanga Bridge and Victorian regulations and licensing requirements must be complied with. Lake Mulwala is designated as New South Wales.

You must have a New South Wales recreational fishing licence to fish in New South Wales whether inland or offshore.

The stretch of river between the Yarrawonga Weir and the Tocumwal Road Bridge is closed to all fishing from 1 September to the 30 November (the Cod spawning season).

A Victorian Recreational Fishing Licence is required for fishing in waters south of the Murray River. Visit the Victorian Department of Primary Industries website, under Fishing & Aquaculture, at www.dpi.vic.gov.au/dpi/index.htm or call 136 186 for further information on fishing or obtaining a fishing licence in Victoria.

PROTECTED FISH

- Murray Cod Closed Season from 1 September to 30 November.
- Murray Crayfish Closed Season from 1 September to 30 April.
- Trout cod are fully protected and must be released immediately if caught accidentally.

For further information contact the Department of Primary Industries, Fisheries Division, Deniliquin on 03 5881 9999.

For general fishing information, call the information line on 1300 550 474 or visit the website at *www.dpi.nsw.gov.au/fisheries*. Please report illegal fishing activities to your local fisheries office or call the Fishers Watch Phoneline on 1800 043 536.

TACKLE SHOPS

here are many speciality tackle shops or general outlets that sell gear and bait in this area—as you would expect of an anglers paradise. The people in these stores are usually aware of what lures or bait are currently producing the best results and they are always ready to pass on the information. Here is a list of the local outlets that can help anglers with tackle or fishing advice—there is always one near to you if you are anywhere along the Murray.

Sportspower Corowa
180 Sanger St
COROWA, NSW
Ph: 02 6033 2155

Howlong Motors
61 Hawkins St
HOWLONG, NSW
Ph: 02 6026 5241

Elk's Hunting & Fishing
582 David St
ALBURY, NSW
Ph: 02 6021 8494

Cohuna Fishing & Camping
1d Cullen St
COHUNA, VIC
Ph: 03 5456 4566

Border Service Station
6 Murray St
BARHAM, NSW
Ph: 03 5453 2306

Echuca Camping
592 High Street
ECHUCA, VIC
Ph: 03 5480 6811

Go Outdoors
117 Lime Avenue
MILDURA, VIC
Ph: 03 5022 8444

Aussie Disposals Mildura
1/79 Langtree Mall
MILDURA, VIC
Ph: 02 5023 6653

Aussie Disposals Albury
546 Olive Street
ALBURY, NSW
Ph: 02 6021 3944

Wingate's Sportz
90 Belmore St
YARRAWONGA, VIC
Ph: 03 5744 1951

Shell Service Station
223 Sanger St
COROWA, NSW
Ph: 02 60333 1030

Bluey's Bait and Tackle
3/65 Thomas Mitchell Drive
WODONGA, VIC
Ph: 02 6056 1259

Masons Tackle
343b Wagga Rd
LAVINGTON, NSW
Ph: 02 6025 1346

Molins BP Service Station
Main St
KOONDROOK, VIC
Ph: 03 5455 2413

Torrumbarry Weir
Holiday Park
835 Weir Rd
TORRUMBARRY, VIC
Ph: 03 5487 7277

Echuca Disposals
598 High Street
ECHUCA, VIC
Ph: 03 5482 3041

Rays Outdoors Mildura
Shop 2/717 Fifteenth Street
MILDURA, VIC
Ph: 03 5021 0100

BCF Albury
Tenancy 13/94 Borella Road
ALBURY, NSW
Ph: 02 6023 6877

Armstrongs Gone Fishing
190 Annesley Street
ECHUCA, VIC
Ph: 03 5482 4291

Intents Fishing & Outdoors
Melbourne St
MULWALA, NSW
Ph: 03 5743 1803

Cappers Pro Tackle
1/62 Thomas Mitchell Dr
WODONGA, VIC
Ph: 02 6024 4029

BP Service Station
163 Main St
RUTHERGLEN, VIC
Ph: 02 6032 8663

BP Service Station
Moulamein Rd
BARHAM, NSW
Ph: 03 5453 2214

Gunbower General Store
& Newsagency
Main St
GUNBOWER, VIC
Ph: 03 5487 1225

Mal's Tacklebox
268 Reilly's Road
YARRAWONGA, VIC
Ph: 03 5743 1711

Willoughby's Outdoor World
73 Thomas Mitchell Drive
WODONGA, VIC
Ph: 02 6056 6188

Rays Outdoors Albury
469 Keiwa Street
ALBURY, NSW
Ph: 02 6023 3789

JC Bait & Tackle
488 Campbell Street
SWAN HILL VIC
Ph: 03 5033 0407

CAMPING THE MURRAY RIVER

There is camping in approximately 70 per cent of the forest adjoining the mighty Murray River. In Victoria where there is no public access to the Murray River other than via private property, camping is NOT permitted on licensed water frontages adjacent to private property.

Parks and reserves along the Victorian side of the Murray River are controlled by Parks Victoria while the New South Wales side is controlled by the Department of Primary Industries—Forest NSW.

Camping along the river ranges from formal campgrounds with facilities to basic bush camping. Some sites have picnic tables and fireplaces for everyone to use, others are just bush camping area. All areas have a risk awareness and this is up to the individual camper, but I will include just a couple.

RISK AWARENESS

- Avoid camping under large river red gums as they can drop branches without warning.
- Swimmers beware, the river has strong current, deep holes and plenty of rock ledges.
- Rope swings can cause very serious injury

RULES

When camping there are a few rules that we all must follow, these rules are there for everyone's safety. If we all follow these few rules the outdoors is great place to be.

CAMPING

- Unless otherwise stated campsites must be at least 20 metres from any waterway.
- Camping is not permitted in designated Day Visitor Areas.
- Permanent structures, leaving caravans or camp on site is not permitted.
- Maintain campsite clean and tidy at all times and remove all rubbish prior to leaving.

TOILETS

- Satisfactory toilet facilities must be provided.
- Portable chemical toilets are recommended.
- Earth toilets must be at least 100 metres from the waterway high bank and must be back filled before leaving with at least 50 cm of earth.

RUBBISH

- Carry in carry out!
- Use bins where provided.
- Don't burn or bury rubbish as animals dig it up.
- Use cans not glass. Glass can cause serious injury.
- Always bring strong rubbish bags with you, so you can take your rubbish home.

It's not hard to have some consideration for your fellow camper as you wouldn't like it to happen to you because is not very good having to pick up someone else rubbish before you set up your camp.

FIRES

- No fires, including gas barbecues, stoves, fridges and lights are to be lit, in the open, on a day of Total Fire Ban. Forests NSW enforces a Solid Fuel Fire Ban (SFFB), generally from October through to March—only gas barbecues may be used in State Forest, except on days of Total Fire Ban (TOBAN).
- Fires must be lit in a properly constructed fire place or in a pit 30 cm deep.
- All flammable material must be cleared around and above for 3 metres and the fire be no larger than 1 metre.
- No fire to be lit within 7.5 metres of any stump or log.
- Fires must not be left unattended at any time .
- Trenches must be back filled and fires must be completely extinguished with water before leaving your campsite.
- Generators should be cleared of all flammable material for 1.5 metres all around.

FIREWOOD

- DON'T cut down any trees live or dead—it is an offence and penalties do apply.
- Bring your own firewood as in some areas supplies are limited on the ground.
- A permit is required to remove wood from allocated areas for domestic use.
- Spray-painting directional arrows and instructions on trees is illegal.

• DOGS AND OTHER PETS

- Dogs are permitted on leads in Gunbower State Forest, but check first in all other areas.

CAMPING AREAS

Here are some general areas that are good to camp in. Some areas are for day visitors only, so there is no camping and some have no vehicle access.

YARRAWONGA TO TOCUMWAL

Regional park downstream of Yarrawonga Caravan Park. This is also known as 'the commons' because of the tent city that materialises during summer.

All sand bars from Yarrawonga to Tocumwal are usually packed over the holiday period with many of the same groups returning year after year.

Dicks Island is a great place but it has no vehicle access, so check them out first.

TOCUMWAL TO PICNIC POINT

- Ulupna Island (many great places to camp.)
- Back of Strathmerton.
- Gulf—Barmah State Forest.

PICNIC POINT TO BARMAH

- Barmah Lakes designated camping area.
- Broken Creek bridge along the forest up to Barmah

BARMAH TO ECHUCA

- Cape Horn.
- Goulburn Junction.
- Bangerang Forest.

ECHUCA TO TORRUMBARRY

- Braun Road area.
- Baillieu Road area.
- Youngs Road area.
- River Road off headwork's road to Torrumbarry Weir. This section has some day visitor only areas.

TORRUMBARRY WEIR TO BARHAM

- Worthy Bend.
- Old Cohuna Headworks.
- Kate Malone Bend.
- Stanton Break.
- Social Bend.
- Nursery Bend 1, 2, 3.
- Cemetery Bend.
- McClure Bend.
- Morton Bend.
- Clump bend.

BARHAM TO MURRABIT

- Hall Lane.
- Bottom Dunbar Road.
- Murrabit ramp area.

MURRABIT TO SWAN HILL (LITTLE MURRAY)

- Hannah Road and Bennett Road.
- Petal Island Junction.
- Brooke Lane.
- The Loddon Floodway.

LITTLE MURRAY RIVER

- End of little Murray road.
- Upstream Swan Hill's Pental Island bridge crossing.

SWAN HILL TO TOOLEYBUC

- Tyntynder River Murray Reserve.
- Nyah—Vinifera River Reserve.
- Nyah—State Forest.
- Wood Wood—Black Stump Bend.

TOOLEYBUC TO ROBINVALE

- State Forest—Wakool Junction.
- State Forest—Murrumbidgee Junction.
- Boundary Bend—Sand Bars.
- State Forest—Yungera Island.
- Knights Bend.

ROBINVALE TO MILDURA

- Happy Valley (River Road–High Bank).
- State Forest—Pound Bend.
- State Forest—KI Bend.
- Kulkyne Forest.
- Bottle Bend.

The Murray River has many great sand bars to camp by, making the water easily accessable.

Pump floats usually indicate a deeper part of the river or small hole – great for bait fishing.

Steve Gaunt from Outlaw Spinnerbait with a healthy trout cod caught on one of his Outlaw Spinnerbaits.

RIVER WATCH

River Watch is a group of concerned authorities made up of police, clubs, boards, councils and community personnel working together to help river users 'Treat the River Like a Friend'. You can report your concerns to River Watch, which will be acted upon with strict confidence. Give description of events, time, date, location and any other information that could help authorities.

For more information check

• NSW. Maritime 131236 general boating information at *www.maritime.nsw.gov.au*

• NSW Fisheries 1300 550 474 or *www.dpi.nsw.gov.au/fisheries*

• Parks Victoria Web at *www.parkweb.vic.gov.au*

• Victoria Fisheries *www.dpi.vic.gov.au/DPI* and select the Fishing and Aquaculture link.

• Emergency Phone Number—for police, ambulance or fire brigade dial 000.

• Mobile phones—You may not be in network range in some areas. To be connected to police, ambulance or fire brigade, key in 112 then press the 'yes' key.

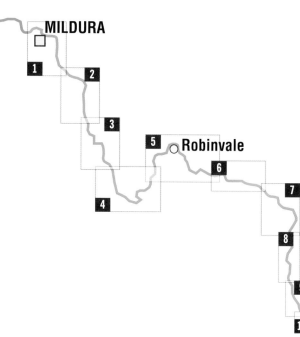

Quick Reference
Map Location Guide
for the Murray River
– Mildura to the Source

MILDURA

Robinvale

Swan Hill

Little Murray River Map

Echuca

1	Mildura to Karadoc	page 14
2	Karadoc to Nangiloc	page 15
3	Nangiloc to KI State Forest	page 16
4	KI State Forest to Euston State Forest	pages 18 & 19
5	Euston State Forest to Manie State Forest	pages 22 & 23
6	Manie State Forest to Narrung	pages 26 & 27
7	Narrung to Kenley	page 28
8	Kenley to Piangil	page 29
9	Piangil to Nyah	page 30
10	Nyah to Beverford	pages 31
11	Beverford to Murraydale	page 32
12	Murraydale to Lake Boga (North)	page 33
13	Lake Boga (North) to Benjeroop Weir	page 36
14	Benjeroop Weir to Murrabit	page 37
15	Murrabit to Barham/Koondrook	pages 38 & 39
	Little Murray River (Marraboor River)	pages 40 & 41
16	Gunbower Creek to McClure Bend	page 42
16A	McClure Bend to Dalley	page 43
17	Dalley Bend to Torrumbarry	page 46
17A	Torrumbarry to Moama State Forest	page 47
18	Moama State Forest to Barmah	pages 48 & 49
19	Barmah Lake to Upstream of Snake Bend	pages 50 & 51
20	Upstream of Snake Bend to Riversdale	pages 52 & 53
21	Riversdale to Barooga	page 54
21A	Barooga to Yarramundee	page 55
22	Yarramundee to Yarrawonga	pages 56 & 57
23	Yarrawonga to Collendina State Forest	pages 58 & 59
24	Collendina State Forest to Howlong	pages 62 & 63
25	Howlong to Wodonga	pages 66 & 67
26	Wodonga to Hume Weir	page 70
27	Lake Hume to Jingelic	pages 72 & 73
28	Jingelic to Tintaldra	pages 76 & 77
29	Tintaldra to Towong Upper	page 81
30	Towong Upper to Hairpin Bend	page 84
31	Hairpin Bend to Tom Groggin	page 86
32	Tom Groggin to Rough Creek	page 88
33	Upper Murray Headwaters	page 89

PART 2

FISHING LOCATIONS

I have been fishing the Murray River for over fifty years and believe I know it quite well. I have fished just about all of it from Mildura to Lake Hume, and Bill Classon has extensively fished the river above Lake Hume. It is not my intention to detail specific places but to give you more of a general idea of the river from Mildura to Lake Hume. Information on some of the other areas I have fished in are also included.

20

9

21

20

21A

22

Yarrawonga

23

24

25

27

28

WODONGA   26   *Lake Hume*

29

Corryong ○   30

31

32

33

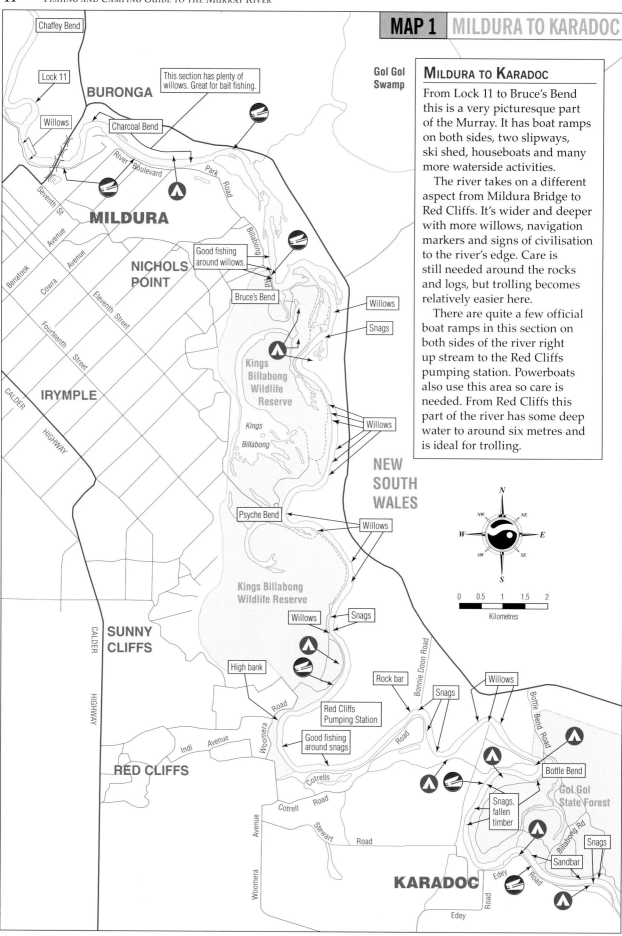

MAP 1   MILDURA TO KARADOC

MILDURA TO KARADOC

From Lock 11 to Bruce's Bend this is a very picturesque part of the Murray. It has boat ramps on both sides, two slipways, ski shed, houseboats and many more waterside activities.

The river takes on a different aspect from Mildura Bridge to Red Cliffs. It's wider and deeper with more willows, navigation markers and signs of civilisation to the river's edge. Care is still needed around the rocks and logs, but trolling becomes relatively easier here.

There are quite a few official boat ramps in this section on both sides of the river right up stream to the Red Cliffs pumping station. Powerboats also use this area so care is needed. From Red Cliffs this part of the river has some deep water to around six metres and is ideal for trolling.

Chaffey Bend

Lock 11

Willows

BURONGA

This section has plenty of willows. Great for bait fishing.

Charcoal Bend

River Boulevard

Park Road

Seventh St

MILDURA

Benatook Avenue

Cowra Avenue

NICHOLS POINT

Eleventh Street

Good fishing around willows.

Billabong Rd

Gol Gol Swamp

Fourteenth Street

Bruce's Bend

Willows

Snags

Kings Billabong Wildlife Reserve

CALDER

IRYMPLE

Kings Billabong

Willows

NEW SOUTH WALES

Psyche Bend

Willows

Kings Billabong Wildlife Reserve

SUNNY CLIFFS

Willows

Snags

High bank

Rock bar

Bonnie Doon Road

Snags

Willows

Woomera Road

Red Cliffs Pumping Station

Good fishing around snags

Road

Bottle Bend Road

CALDER HIGHWAY

Indi Avenue

RED CLIFFS

Cotrells Road

Cotrell Road

Avenue

Stewart Road

Road

Bottle Bend

Gol Gol State Forest

Snags, fallen timber

Billabong Rd

Snags

Sandbar

KARADOC

Edey Road

Woomera Road

Edey

N
NW · NE
W · E
SW · SE
S

0   0.5   1   1.5   2
Kilometres

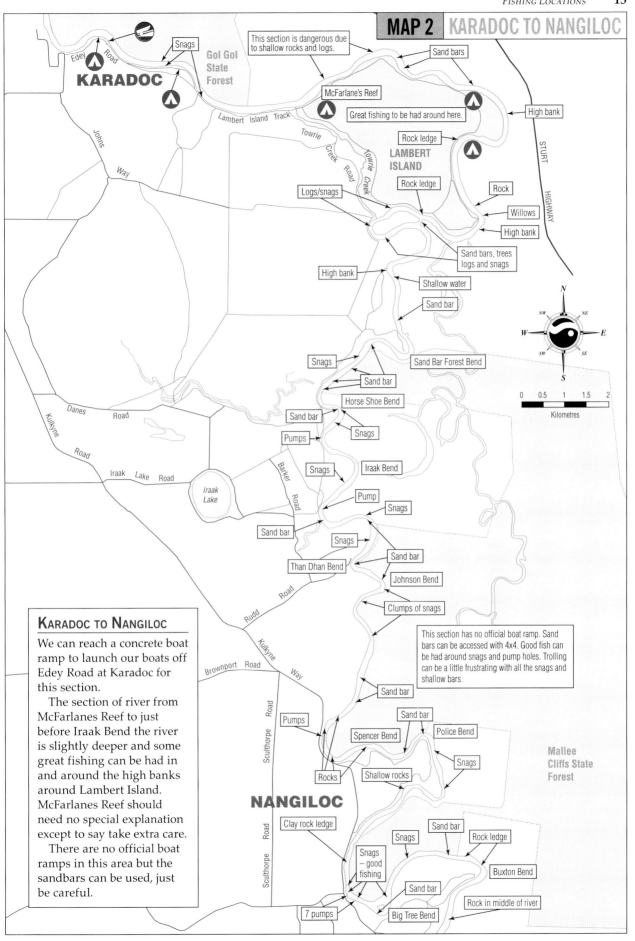

MAP 2 KARADOC TO NANGILOC

Snags

Edey Road

Gol Gol State Forest

This section is dangerous due to shallow rocks and logs.

Sand bars

KARADOC

Lambert Island Track

McFarlane's Reef

Great fishing to be had around here.

High bank

STURT HIGHWAY

Towrie Creek

Rock ledge

LAMBERT ISLAND

Johns Way

Towrie Creek Road

Rock ledge

Rock

Logs/snags

Willows

High bank

Sand bars, trees logs and snags

High bank

Shallow water

Sand bar

Sand Bar Forest Bend

N
NW NE
W E
SW SE
S

Snags

Sand bar

Danes Road

Horse Shoe Bend

Sand bar

Snags

Kulkyne Road

Pumps

Iraak Bend

Iraak Lake Road

Snags

Barker Road

Iraak Lake

Pump

Snags

Sand bar

Snags

Sand bar

Than Dhan Bend

Johnson Bend

Road

Clumps of snags

Rudd Road

This section has no official boat ramp. Sand bars can be accessed with 4x4. Good fish can be had around snags and pump holes. Trolling can be a little frustrating with all the snags and shallow bars.

0 0.5 1 1.5 2
Kilometres

KARADOC TO NANGILOC

We can reach a concrete boat ramp to launch our boats off Edey Road at Karadoc for this section.

The section of river from McFarlanes Reef to just before Iraak Bend the river is slightly deeper and some great fishing can be had in and around the high banks around Lambert Island. McFarlanes Reef should need no special explanation except to say take extra care.

There are no official boat ramps in this area but the sandbars can be used, just be careful.

Brownport Road

Kulkyne Way

Sand bar

Sculthorpe Road

Pumps

Sand bar

Spencer Bend

Police Bend

NANGILOC

Snags

Rocks

Shallow rocks

Mallee Cliffs State Forest

Sculthorpe Road

Clay rock ledge

Snags

Sand bar

Rock ledge

Snags – good fishing

Buxton Bend

Sand bar

7 pumps

Big Tree Bend

Rock in middle of river

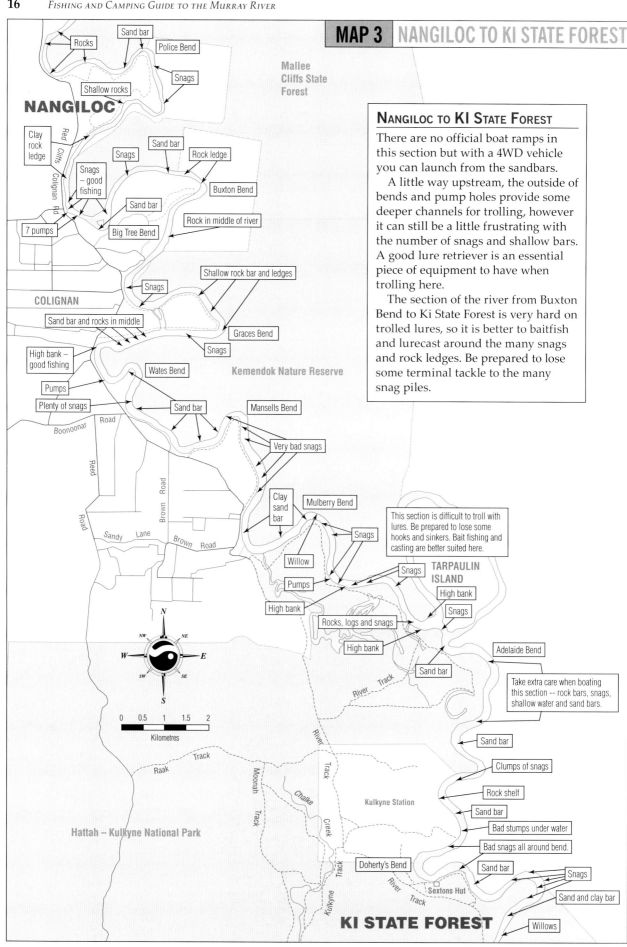

MAP 3 NANGILOC TO KI STATE FOREST

Rocks

Sand bar

Police Bend

Snags

Shallow rocks

NANGILOC

Mallee Cliffs State Forest

Clay rock ledge

Red Cliffs

Colignan Rd

Snags

Sand bar

Rock ledge

Snags – good fishing

Buxton Bend

7 pumps

Sand bar

Big Tree Bend

Rock in middle of river

COLIGNAN

Snags

Shallow rock bar and ledges

Sand bar and rocks in middle

Graces Bend

Snags

High bank – good fishing

Wates Bend

Kemendok Nature Reserve

Pumps

Plenty of snags

Boonoonar Road

Sand bar

Mansells Bend

Very bad snags

Reed Road

Brown Road

Sandy Lane

Brown Road

Clay sand bar

Mulberry Bend

Snags

Willow

Pumps

High bank

This section is difficult to troll with lures. Be prepared to lose some hooks and sinkers. Bait fishing and casting are better suited here.

Snags

TARPAULIN ISLAND

High bank

Snags

Rocks, logs and snags

High bank

Sand bar

Adelaide Bend

Take extra care when boating this section -- rock bars, snags, shallow water and sand bars.

N
NW NE
W E
SW SE
S

0 0.5 1 1.5 2
Kilometres

River Track

River Track

Raak Track

Moonah Track

Chalke Creek

Kulkyne Station

Sand bar

Clumps of snags

Rock shelf

Sand bar

Bad stumps under water

Bad snags all around bend.

Hattah – Kulkyne National Park

Kulkyne Track

River Track

Doherty's Bend

Sextons Hut

Sand bar

Snags

Sand and clay bar

KI STATE FOREST

Willows

Nangiloc to KI State Forest

There are no official boat ramps in this section but with a 4WD vehicle you can launch from the sandbars.

A little way upstream, the outside of bends and pump holes provide some deeper channels for trolling, however it can still be a little frustrating with the number of snags and shallow bars. A good lure retriever is an essential piece of equipment to have when trolling here.

The section of the river from Buxton Bend to Ki State Forest is very hard on trolled lures, so it is better to baitfish and lurecast around the many snags and rock ledges. Be prepared to lose some terminal tackle to the many snag piles.

ABOVE: Ashley Hinson caught this good sized Murray cod on a StumpJumper lure.

ABOVE: This Murray cray is intent on making its escape!

LEFT: Black water Murray crays.

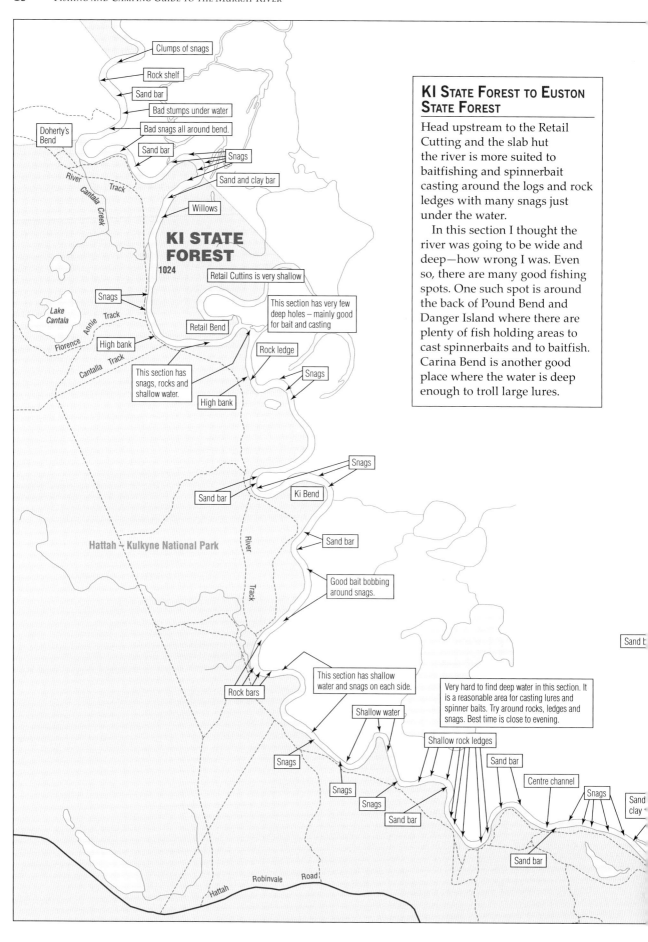

Clumps of snags

Rock shelf

Sand bar

Bad stumps under water

Bad snags all around bend.

Doherty's Bend

Sand bar

Snags

Sand and clay bar

River Cantala Track

Cantala Creek

Willows

KI STATE FOREST

1024

Lake Cantala

Snags

Annie Track

Florence

Cantalla Track

High bank

Retail Bend

Retail Cuttins is very shallow

This section has very few deep holes – mainly good for bait and casting

This section has snags, rocks and shallow water.

High bank

Rock ledge

Snags

High bank

KI STATE FOREST TO EUSTON STATE FOREST

Head upstream to the Retail Cutting and the slab hut the river is more suited to baitfishing and spinnerbait casting around the logs and rock ledges with many snags just under the water.

In this section I thought the river was going to be wide and deep—how wrong I was. Even so, there are many good fishing spots. One such spot is around the back of Pound Bend and Danger Island where there are plenty of fish holding areas to cast spinnerbaits and to baitfish. Carina Bend is another good place where the water is deep enough to troll large lures.

Snags

Sand bar

Ki Bend

Hattah – Kulkyne National Park

River

Track

Sand bar

Good bait bobbing around snags.

This section has shallow water and snags on each side.

Rock bars

Shallow water

Very hard to find deep water in this section. It is a reasonable area for casting lures and spinner baits. Try around rocks, ledges and snags. Best time is close to evening.

Snags

Shallow rock ledges

Sand bar

Centre channel

Snags

Sand b

Sand clay

Snags

Snags

Sand bar

Sand bar

Hattah Robinvale Road

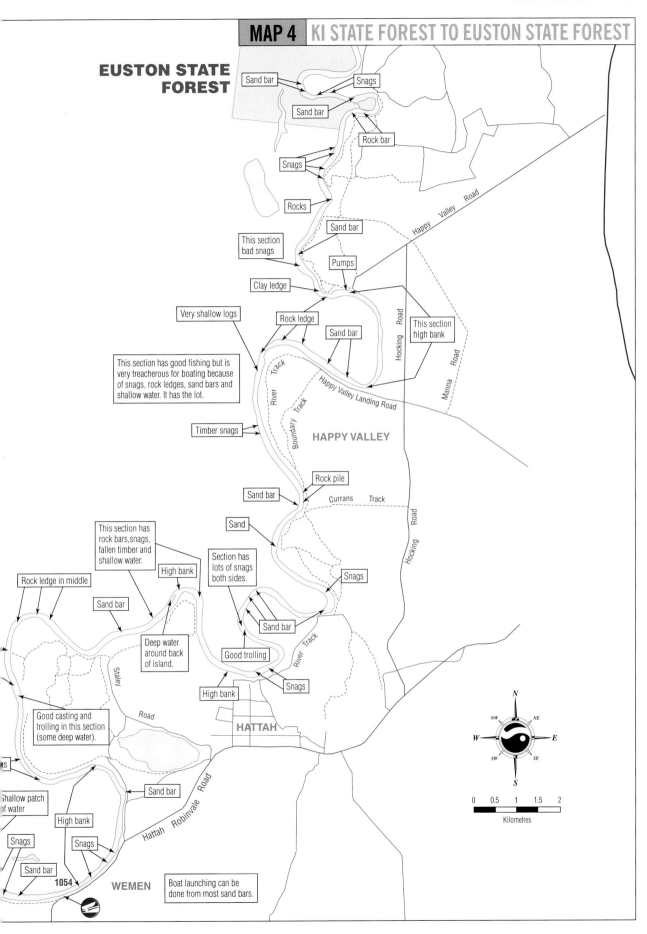

MAP 4 KI STATE FOREST TO EUSTON STATE FOREST

EUSTON STATE FOREST

Sand bar

Snags

Sand bar

Rock bar

Snags

Rocks

Happy Valley Road

Sand bar

This section bad snags

Pumps

Clay ledge

Rock ledge

Very shallow logs

Sand bar

This section high bank

Hocking Road

Manna Road

This section has good fishing but is very treacherous for boating because of snags, rock ledges, sand bars and shallow water. It has the lot.

River Track

Boundary Track

Happy Valley Landing Road

Timber snags

HAPPY VALLEY

Rock pile

Sand bar

Currans Track

Sand

This section has rock bars, snags, fallen timber and shallow water.

High bank

Section has lots of snags both sides.

Snags

Hocking Road

Rock ledge in middle

Sand bar

Deep water around back of island.

Good trolling

Sand bar

River Track

Staley Road

Good casting and trolling in this section (some deep water).

High bank

Snags

HATTAH

Sand bar

Hattah Robinvale Road

Shallow patch of water

High bank

Snags

Snags

Sand bar

1054

WEMEN

Boat launching can be done from most sand bars.

N
NW NE
W E
SW SE
S

0   0.5   1   1.5   2
Kilometres

RIGHT: Downstream from Weir No. 15.

LEFT: River Murray cliffs at Euston.

MURRAY – DARLING BASIN COMMISSION

WEIR & LOCK № 15
EUSTON
DISTANCE FROM RIVER MOUTH, 1,110 km
HEIGHT OF POOL ABOVE SEA LEVEL, 47·60ᴹ
CONSTRUCTION COMPLETED, 1937

ABOVE: Weir No. 15 at Euston

MAP 5 EUSTON STATE FOREST TO MANIE STATE FOREST

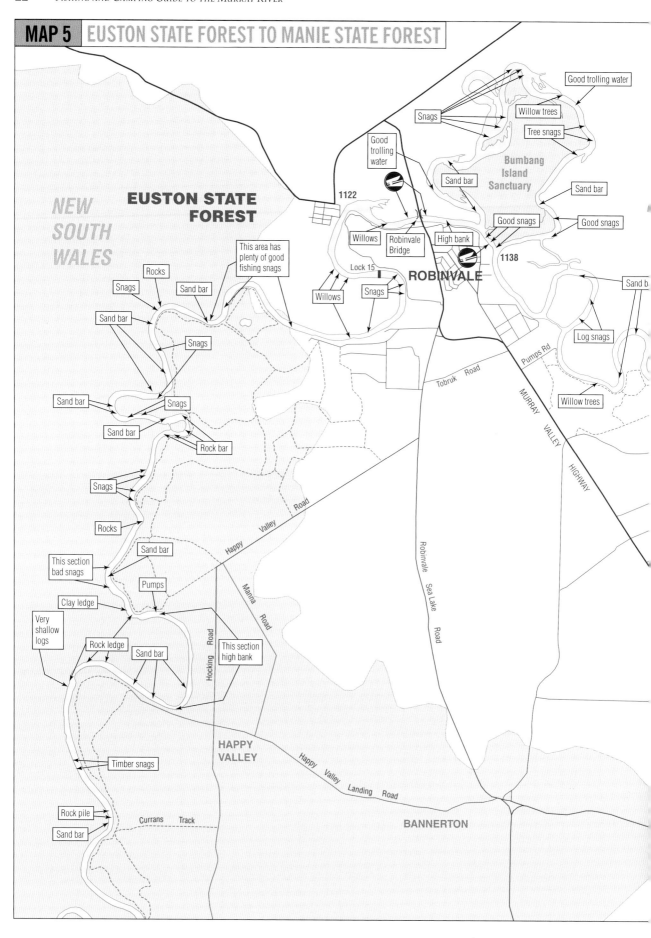

NEW
SOUTH
WALES

EUSTON STATE
FOREST

Good trolling water

Snags

Willow trees

Tree snags

Good trolling water

Bumbang
Island
Sanctuary

Sand bar

Sand bar

1122

Willows

Robinvale
Bridge

High bank

Good snags

Good snags

1138

This area has
plenty of good
fishing snags

Rocks

Snags

Sand bar

Lock 15

ROBINVALE

Sand b

Sand bar

Willows

Snags

Snags

Log snags

Sand bar

Snags

Pumps Rd

Willow trees

Sand bar

Snags

Rock bar

Tobruk   Road

Snags

Rocks

Robinvale   Sea Lake   Road

MURRAY   VALLEY   HIGHWAY

Happy   Valley   Road

Sand bar

This section
bad snags

Pumps

Manna   Road

Clay ledge

Hocking   Road

Very
shallow
logs

Rock ledge

Sand bar

This section
high bank

HAPPY
VALLEY

Timber snags

Happy   Valley   Landing   Road

Rock pile

BANNERTON

Sand bar

Currans   Track

ABOVE: River Murray at Robinvale

EUSTON STATE FOREST TO MANIE STATE FOREST

There is a boat ramp beside the pump and willow trees opposite the Bumbang Island sanctuary at marker 1138.

As they get closer to Robinvale from Happy Valley, boats need to take care because of the rock bars, snag piles and other obstructions in the water. Robinvale has more boat launching facilities around the bridge.

In this section you will notice the scenery is always changing—high banks, willows, rock bars, sand bars, clay bars and lots of pump holes—what a place to go fishing. This is one of the most picturesque sections I have fished in for a long time. It has deep water for trolling and plenty of snags and rock ledges for baitfishing and lurecasting. Further upstream, around 1176, you have deep water, rocks, snags, willow trees and sand bars. With a boat ramp at the junction of Bonvaricall Creek, this area has everything you need.

This section has everything for the fisherman. From over hanging willows to plenty of snags with slow and fast running water. It's also a wider section of the Murray with deeper water.

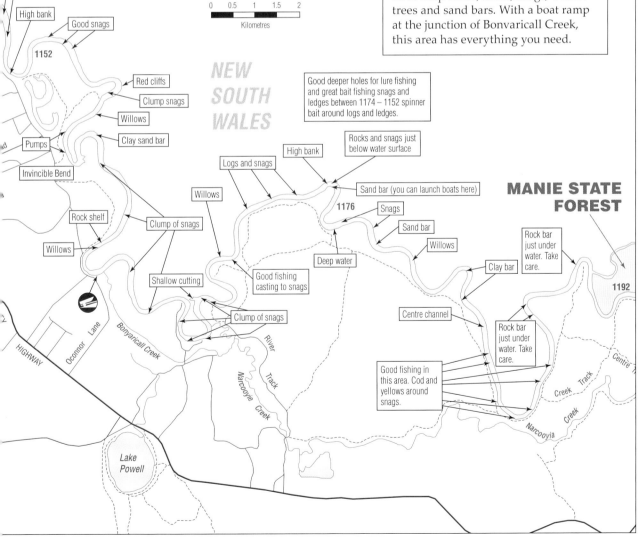

N
NW   NE
W   E
SW   SE
S

0   0.5   1   1.5   2
Kilometres

NEW SOUTH WALES

SOUTH S

Snags

High bank

Good snags

1152

Red cliffs

Clump snags

Willows

Clay sand bar

Pumps

Invincible Bend

Rock shelf

Clump of snags

Willows

Shallow cutting

Clump of snags

Good deeper holes for lure fishing and great bait fishing snags and ledges between 1174 – 1152 spinner bait around logs and ledges.

Logs and snags

High bank

Rocks and snags just below water surface

Sand bar (you can launch boats here)

1176

Snags

Sand bar

Willows

Willows

Deep water

Good fishing casting to snags

Clay bar

MANIE STATE FOREST

Rock bar just under water. Take care.

1192

Centre channel

Rock bar just under water. Take care.

Good fishing in this area. Cod and yellows around snags.

HIGHWAY

Oconnor Lane

Bonvaricall Creek

River Track

Narcooyie Creek

Creek Track

Narcooyia Creek

Centre Tr

Lake Powell

RIGHT: Robinvale road bridge.

LEFT, BELOW AND BOTTOM: Murray River views in the Robinvale area

ABOVE: Boundary Bend

MANIE STATE FOREST TO NARRUNG

Langs Bend has plenty of rock ledges and high banks, and fishes well. From the Buchanans Lane all around Buchanans Bend there is great fishing of all types—trolling, lurecasting and baitfishing. Care when boating is still needed because of all the hidden dangers of rock ledges and snags.

Towards Boundary Bend we find numerous good fish holding areas all worth a little time.

There is a boat ramp beside the Murray Valley Highway at Boundary Bend, which is okay for the trailer boats.

Around marker 1242 is the Murrumbidgee Junction where the river is a very fishy and is worth spending time to flick some lures or spinnerbaits around.

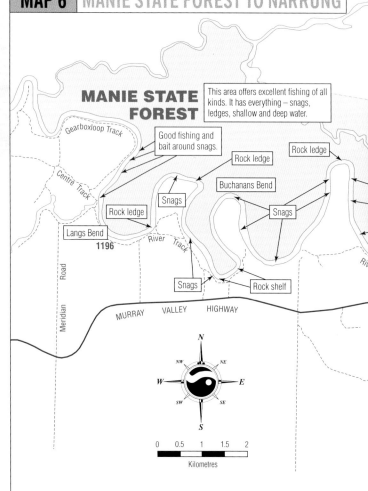

MAP 6   MANIE STATE FOREST TO NARRUNG

MANIE STATE FOREST

This area offers excellent fishing of all kinds. It has everything – snags, ledges, shallow and deep water.

Gearboxloop Track

Good fishing and bait around snags.

Rock ledge

Rock ledge

Centre Track

Buchanans Bend

Snags

Rock ledge

Langs Bend
1196

River Track

Snags

River

Snags

Rock shelf

Meridian   Road

MURRAY   VALLEY   HIGHWAY

N
NW   NE
W   E
SW   SE
S

0   0.5   1   1.5   2
Kilometres

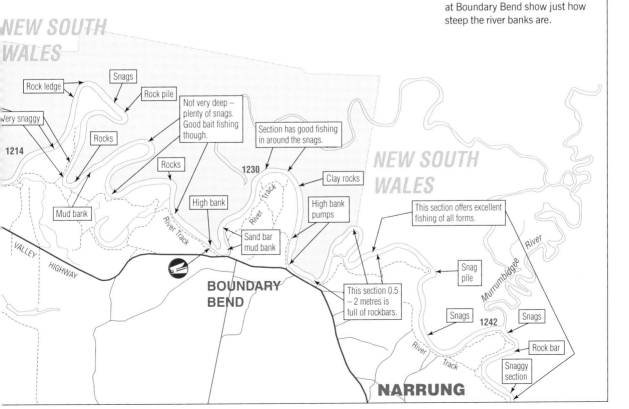

NEW SOUTH WALES

Rock ledge

Snags

Rock pile

Not very deep – plenty of snags. Good bait fishing though.

Section has good fishing in around the snags.

Very snaggy

Rocks

1214

Rocks

1230

Clay rocks

NEW SOUTH WALES

Mud bank

High bank

High bank pumps

This section offers excellent fishing of all forms.

River Track

River Track

Sand bar mud bank

VALLEY HIGHWAY

BOUNDARY BEND

This section 0.5 – 2 metres is full of rockbars.

Snag pile

Murrumbidgee River

Snags

1242

Snags

River Track

Rock bar

Snaggy section

NARRUNG

MAP 7 NARRUNG TO KENLEY

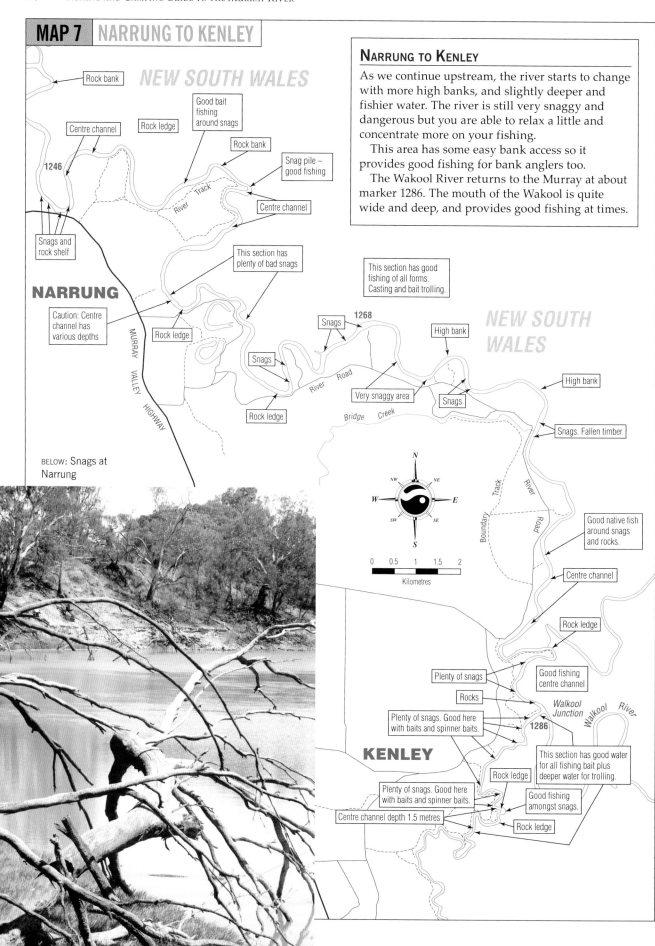

NEW SOUTH WALES

Rock bank

Centre channel

Rock ledge

Good bait fishing around snags

Rock bank

1246

Snag pile – good fishing

River Track

Centre channel

Snags and rock shelf

This section has plenty of bad snags

NARRUNG

Caution: Centre channel has various depths

Rock ledge

Rock ledge

MURRAY VALLEY HIGHWAY

BELOW: Snags at Narrung

NARRUNG TO KENLEY

As we continue upstream, the river starts to change with more high banks, and slightly deeper and fishier water. The river is still very snaggy and dangerous but you are able to relax a little and concentrate more on your fishing.

This area has some easy bank access so it provides good fishing for bank anglers too.

The Wakool River returns to the Murray at about marker 1286. The mouth of the Wakool is quite wide and deep, and provides good fishing at times.

This section has good fishing of all forms. Casting and bait trolling.

Snags

1268

High bank

NEW SOUTH WALES

Snags

Very snaggy area

High bank

Snags

Rock ledge

River Road

Bridge Creek

Snags. Fallen timber

Boundary Track

River Road

Good native fish around snags and rocks.

N
NW NE
W E
SW SE
S

0 0.5 1 1.5 2
Kilometres

Centre channel

Rock ledge

Plenty of snags

Good fishing centre channel

Rocks

Walkool Junction

Walkool River

Plenty of snags. Good here with baits and spinner baits.

1286

KENLEY

This section has good water for all fishing bait plus deeper water for trolling.

Plenty of snags. Good here with baits and spinner baits.

Rock ledge

Good fishing amongst snags.

Centre channel depth 1.5 metres

Rock ledge

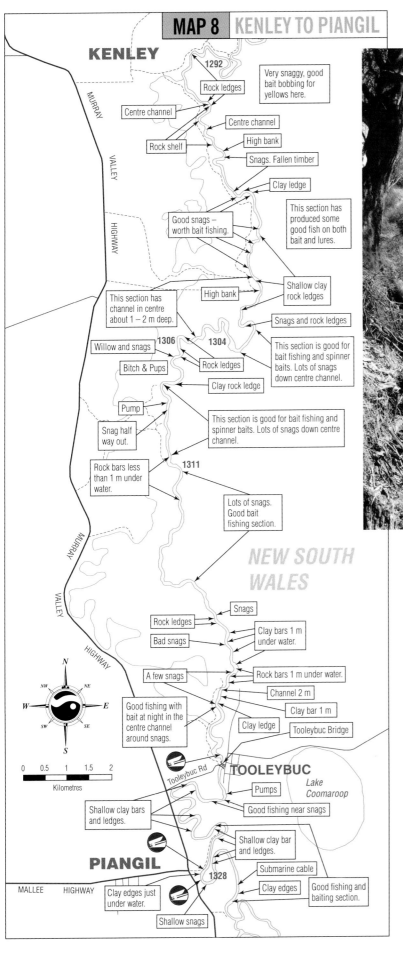

MAP 8 KENLEY TO PIANGIL

KENLEY

MURRAY VALLEY HIGHWAY

1292

Rock ledges

Very snaggy, good bait bobbing for yellows here.

Centre channel

Centre channel

Rock shelf

High bank

Snags. Fallen timber

Clay ledge

Good snags – worth bait fishing.

This section has produced some good fish on both bait and lures.

High bank

Shallow clay rock ledges

This section has channel in centre about 1 – 2 m deep.

Snags and rock ledges

1306

1304

Willow and snags

Bitch & Pups

Rock ledges

This section is good for bait fishing and spinner baits. Lots of snags down centre channel.

Clay rock ledge

Pump

This section is good for bait fishing and spinner baits. Lots of snags down centre channel.

Snag half way out.

Rock bars less than 1 m under water.

1311

Lots of snags. Good bait fishing section.

NEW SOUTH WALES

MURRAY VALLEY HIGHWAY

Rock ledges

Bad snags

Snags

Clay bars 1 m under water.

A few snags

Rock bars 1 m under water.

Channel 2 m

Good fishing with bait at night in the centre channel around snags.

Clay bar 1 m

Clay ledge

Tooleybuc Bridge

N NW NE W E SW SE S

Tooleybuc Rd

TOOLEYBUC

Lake Coomaroop

0 0.5 1 1.5 2
Kilometres

Pumps

Good fishing near snags

Shallow clay bars and ledges.

Shallow clay bar and ledges.

PIANGIL

1328

Submarine cable

MALLEE HIGHWAY

Clay edges just under water.

Clay edges

Good fishing and baiting section.

Shallow snags

ABOVE: River Murray at Wood Wood.

KENLEY TO PIANGIL

After passing the rock bars that are just under the water—called the Bitch and Pups—there is good fishing to be had around the high banks and ledges for both bait and lure fishing.

From around marker 1306 to 1311 care is needed as rock bars protrude from the water and others are less than one metre under water. Snags and clay ledges extend to over half way across the river.

After passing under the Tooleybuc Road Bridge you come to a new boat ramp that has been put in around 1328 for public use. It should get a lot of use as this area has produced some excellent catches in the past to baitfishing and lurecasting around the clay ledges and many snags. Just upstream of 1330 are submarine cables, so take care and look out for the signs.

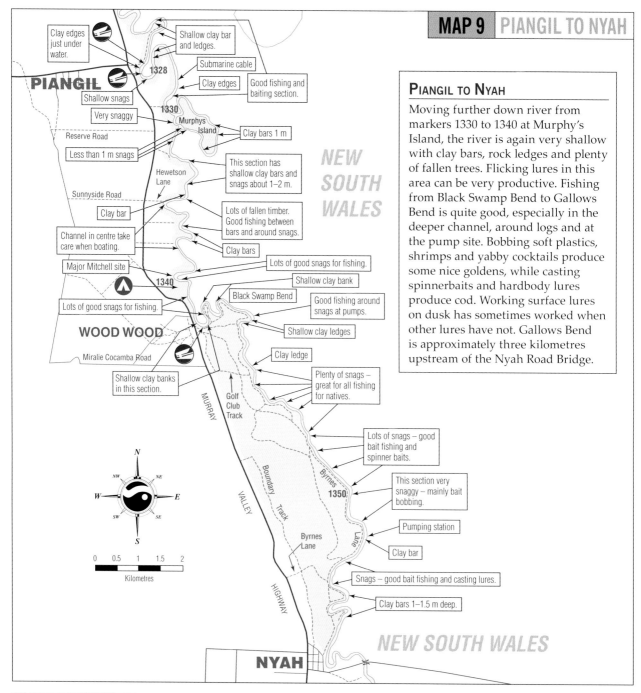

MAP 9   PIANGIL TO NYAH

Clay edges just under water.

Shallow clay bar and ledges.

Submarine cable

1328

Clay edges

PIANGIL

Good fishing and baiting section.

Shallow snags

1330

Very snaggy

Murphys Island

Reserve Road

Clay bars 1 m

Less than 1 m snags

Hewetson Lane

This section has shallow clay bars and snags about 1–2 m.

Sunnyside Road

Clay bar

Lots of fallen timber. Good fishing between bars and around snags.

Channel in centre take care when boating.

Clay bars

Major Mitchell site

Lots of good snags for fishing.

1340

Lots of good snags for fishing.

Shallow clay bank

Black Swamp Bend

Good fishing around snags at pumps.

WOOD WOOD

Shallow clay ledges

Miralie Cocamba Road

Clay ledge

Shallow clay banks in this section.

Golf Club Track

Plenty of snags – great for all fishing for natives.

MURRAY

Boundary Track

VALLEY

Lots of snags – good bait fishing and spinner baits.

Byrnes

This section very snaggy – mainly bait bobbing.

1350

Byrnes Lane

Pumping station

Byrnes Lane

Clay bar

HIGHWAY

Snags – good bait fishing and casting lures.

Clay bars 1–1.5 m deep.

NEW SOUTH WALES

NYAH

NEW SOUTH WALES

N
NW NE
W E
SW SE
S

0   0.5   1   1.5   2
Kilometres

PIANGIL TO NYAH

Moving further down river from markers 1330 to 1340 at Murphy's Island, the river is again very shallow with clay bars, rock ledges and plenty of fallen trees. Flicking lures in this area can be very productive. Fishing from Black Swamp Bend to Gallows Bend is quite good, especially in the deeper channel, around logs and at the pump site. Bobbing soft plastics, shrimps and yabby cocktails produce some nice goldens, while casting spinnerbaits and hardbody lures produce cod. Working surface lures on dusk has sometimes worked when other lures have not. Gallows Bend is approximately three kilometres upstream of the Nyah Road Bridge.

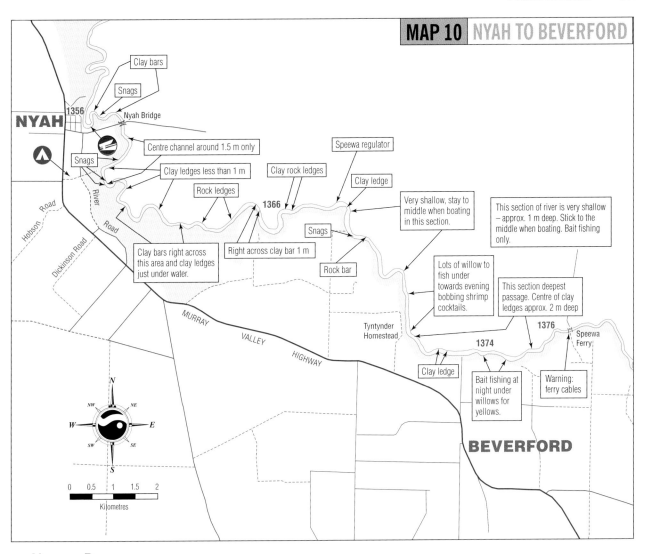

MAP 10 NYAH TO BEVERFORD

Clay bars

Snags

1356

NYAH

Nyah Bridge

Centre channel around 1.5 m only

Snags

Clay ledges less than 1 m

Speewa regulator

Clay rock ledges

Clay ledge

Rock ledges

1366

Very shallow, stay to middle when boating in this section.

This section of river is very shallow – approx. 1 m deep. Stick to the middle when boating. Bait fishing only.

Snags

Clay bars right across this area and clay ledges just under water.

Right across clay bar 1 m

Rock bar

Lots of willow to fish under towards evening bobbing shrimp cocktails.

This section deepest passage. Centre of clay ledges approx. 2 m deep

1376

Speewa Ferry

Tyntynder Homestead

1374

Warning: ferry cables

Clay ledge

Bait fishing at night under willows for yellows.

MURRAY VALLEY HIGHWAY

BEVERFORD

Hobson Road

Dickinson Road

River Road

N NW NE W E SW SE S

0 0.5 1 1.5 2
Kilometres

NYAH TO BEVERFORD

The water on both sides of the boat ramp at the Nyah Bridge is very shallow, so extra care is needed when launching and travelling this section of the river. There are still plenty of good places for the dedicated angler to baitfish and spinnerbait around the many snags and rocks. Care must be taken when approaching Tyntynder Homestead because of the clay and rock ledges which spread right across the river.

Further upstream, just before the Speewa Ferry, there is good fishing to be had under the willows towards evening. This section of the Murray River is not very deep, so it is wise to stay in the centre channel. Remain alert for signs warning of ferry cables.

LEFT: There is good baitfishing to be found under willows.

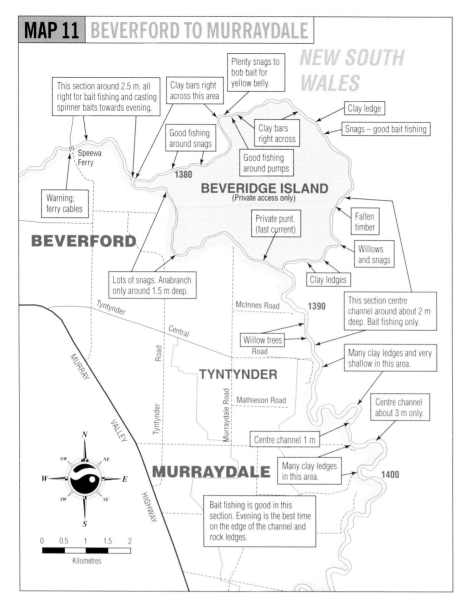

MAP 11 BEVERFORD TO MURRAYDALE

NEW SOUTH WALES

This section around 2.5 m, all right for bait fishing and casting spinner baits towards evening.

Plenty snags to bob bait for yellow belly.

Clay bars right across this area

Good fishing around snags

Clay bars right across

Clay ledge

Snags – good bait fishing

Good fishing around pumps

Speewa Ferry

1380

BEVERIDGE ISLAND
(Private access only)

Warning: ferry cables

Private punt. (fast current)

Fallen timber

Willows and snags

BEVERFORD

Lots of snags. Anabranch only around 1.5 m deep.

Clay ledges

Tyntynder

McInnes Road

1390

This section centre channel around about 2 m deep. Bait fishing only.

Central

Willow trees Road

Many clay ledges and very shallow in this area.

TYNTYNDER

Mathieson Road

Centre channel about 3 m only.

Centre channel 1 m

MURRAYDALE

Many clay ledges in this area.

1400

Bait fishing is good in this section. Evening is the best time on the edge of the channel and rock ledges.

MURRAY VALLEY HIGHWAY

Tyntynder Road

Murraydale Road

N NW NE W E SW SE S

0 0.5 1 1.5 2
Kilometres

BEVERFORD TO MURRAYDALE

A little further upriver you come to Beveridge Island. Be careful of the private punt crossing as the anabranch around here has a fast current.

Some good fish have been caught here in the Murray along the willows and fallen timber. Casting spinnerbaits or small hardbody lures and bobbing baits are worth trying right around the island.

You can become a little complacent when boating in this area as the river becomes a little wider, but not deeper. The centre channel varies in depth from one to three metres and has many very shallow clay rock edges that can damage your boat and motor. Baitfishing and spinnerbaiting for natives towards evening is the way to fish around Tyntynder.

BELOW: Fallen timber has great potential for casting spinnerbaits, small hardbody lures and bobbing baits.

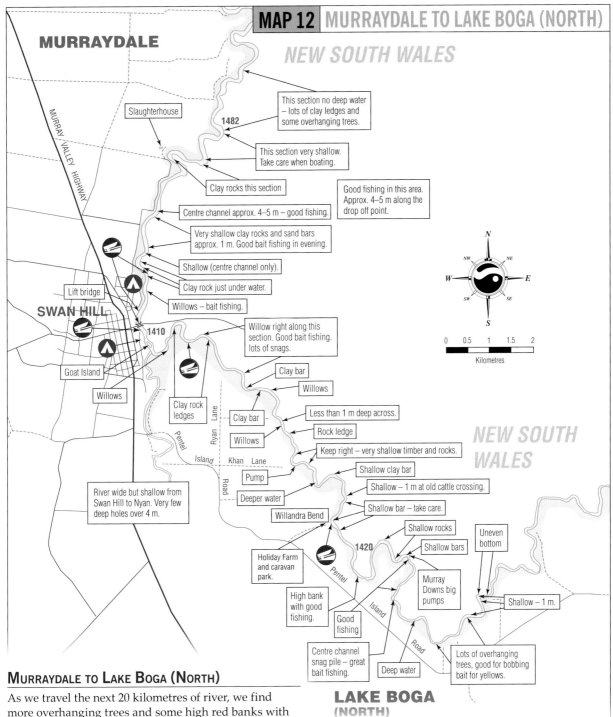

MAP 12 MURRAYDALE TO LAKE BOGA (NORTH)

MURRAYDALE

NEW SOUTH WALES

Slaughterhouse

1482

This section no deep water – lots of clay ledges and some overhanging trees.

This section very shallow. Take care when boating.

Clay rocks this section

Centre channel approx. 4–5 m – good fishing.

Good fishing in this area. Approx. 4–5 m along the drop off point.

Very shallow clay rocks and sand bars approx. 1 m. Good bait fishing in evening.

Shallow (centre channel only).

Lift bridge

Clay rock just under water.

Willows – bait fishing.

SWAN HILL

Willow right along this section. Good bait fishing, lots of snags.

1410

Clay bar

Willows

Goat Island

Clay rock ledges

Clay bar

Less than 1 m deep across.

Willows

Ryan Lane

Willows

Rock ledge

Keep right – very shallow timber and rocks.

NEW SOUTH WALES

Pentel Island

Khan Lane

Pump

Shallow clay bar

Shallow – 1 m at old cattle crossing.

Deeper water

Shallow bar – take care.

Ryan Road

Willandra Bend

Shallow rocks

Uneven bottom

River wide but shallow from Swan Hill to Nyan. Very few deep holes over 4 m.

1420

Shallow bars

Murray Downs big pumps

Shallow – 1 m.

Holiday Farm and caravan park

High bank with good fishing.

Good fishing

Pentel Island Road

Murray Downs big pumps

Centre channel snag pile – great bait fishing.

Deep water

Lots of overhanging trees, good for bobbing bait for yellows.

N NE NW W E SW SE S

0   0.5   1   1.5   2
Kilometres

MURRAYDALE TO LAKE BOGA (NORTH)

As we travel the next 20 kilometres of river, we find more overhanging trees and some high red banks with a deeper channel running down the centre of the river. These areas are great places for all kinds of fishing.

Upstream we come to the slaughterhouse. For about two kilometres either side is some deeper water that provides great fishing.

The river widens before Swan Hill but it has very few places over four metres deep. As you approach Swan Hill you pass two of the town's boat ramps. Fishing around the willows between these ramps has produced some great native fish.

We notice the tranquillity of the river is overtaken by civilisation, but there are still some great areas to wet a line within the city limits. The Little Murray rejoins

LAKE BOGA (NORTH)

the river just upstream of Goat Island in a shallow area where care needs to be taken. Care must also be taken because paddleboats operate on the river at Swan Hill.

When boating from here you need to be very careful of the rock bars. One place just upstream of the Willandra Bend was an old cattle crossing and the water is only one metre deep. A little further upriver we have the boat ramp at the holiday farm caravan park around Willandra Bend. There are some deeper holes around the pump site, the willows and on the outside of bends that are suitable for baitfishing. A depth sounder is very useful around this section.

ABOVE: River Murray at Swan Hill

ABOVE LEFT: Pyapp, Swan Hill

LEFT: Swan Hill road bridge.

BELOW: River Murray at Swan Hill

Lake Boga (North) to Benjeroop Weir

Although this section of river is slightly deeper, there are still many traps for the unsuspecting boater. We start to come across some overhanging trees (willows) that provide excellent baitfishing and lurecasting.

This section of the river is very popular but again, camping places are limited due to no public access except via private property and no camping allowed on the private property. On Pental Island around marker

1454 there are a few boat ramps that are suitable for larger boats.

As we approach Benjeroop Weir, the river becomes shallow with plenty of downed timber and rock ledges. These are great places for bobbing bait and using small lures towards evening. Numerous golden perch and Murray cod have been caught in this section of the river.

MAP 13   LAKE BOGA (NORTH) TO BENJEROOP WEIR

NEW SOUTH WALES

This section is good for bait and spinner bait.

Shallow bar

Plenty of snags

Centre channel swift current.

1432

Shallows

Fallen timber

Bait fishing

Clay

Lots of logs (golden perch fishing bait bobbing)

Good fishing this section

Fallen timber

Strong current centre and deeper channel.

Good lure fishing

Funnel Bend

Very snaggy

Clay dirt ramp

No public access except via private property. No camping.

Swift current

1442

Shallow bar

Shallow ledge

Willows overhang and very rocky. Extra care needed.

Rock bar

Good fishing bait casting

Ledge clay rocks

Shallow bar

Good bait and lure fishing – good over hanging trees.

LAKE BOGA (NORTH)

Over hanging trees – good bait fishing.

No public access except via private property. No camping.

1454 Shallow bar

Fallen timber – good bait fishing.

Good water for all fishing with plenty of snags.

Good fishing around over hanging trees and willows.

Pentel Island Pump Station

BENJEROOP WEIR

Benjerc Weir

Old pump station

Little Murray River

BELOW: Pental Island Bridge

See pages 40 & 41 for the complete Little Murray River map

MAP 14 BENJEROOP WEIR TO MURRABIT

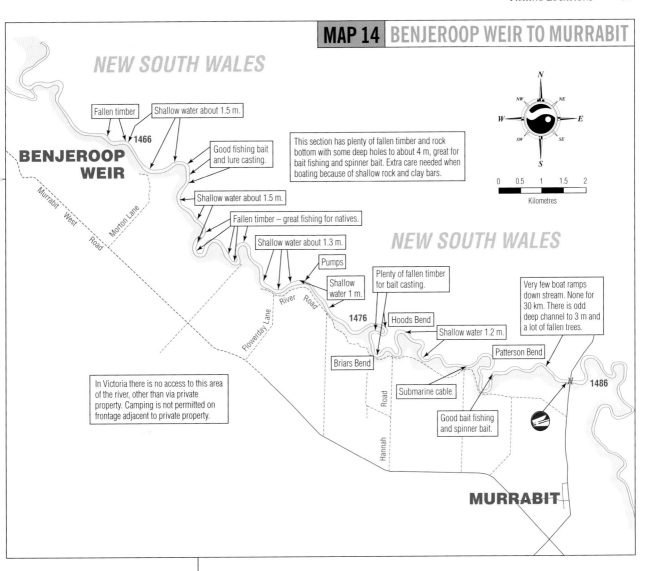

NEW SOUTH WALES

BENJEROOP WEIR

Fallen timber

Shallow water about 1.5 m.

1466

Good fishing bait and lure casting.

Murrabit West Road

Morton Lane

Shallow water about 1.5 m.

Fallen timber – great fishing for natives.

Shallow water about 1.3 m.

Pumps

Shallow water 1 m.

This section has plenty of fallen timber and rock bottom with some deep holes to about 4 m, great for bait fishing and spinner bait. Extra care needed when boating because of shallow rock and clay bars.

NEW SOUTH WALES

1476

Plenty of fallen timber for bait casting.

Hoods Bend

Shallow water 1.2 m.

Very few boat ramps down stream. None for 30 km. There is odd deep channel to 3 m and a lot of fallen trees.

Patterson Bend

1486

Briars Bend

Submarine cable

Good bait fishing and spinner bait.

River Road

Flowerday Lane

Road

Hannah

In Victoria there is no access to this area of the river, other than via private property. Camping is not permitted on frontage adjacent to private property.

MURRABIT

0 0.5 1 1.5 2
Kilometres

Good fishing at night 2 m plus.

Clay rocks and snags section good for small lures and baits.

Good bait fishing.

Shallow water about 1.5 m.

Good for lure casting and trolling small lures.

3 m deep – good fishing.

1466

Morton Road

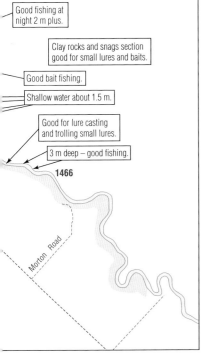

BENJEROOP WEIR TO MURRABIT

As you move towards the Benjeroop Weir (Little Murray Weir) the river becomes a little deeper and there are sections that can be trolled with great success using medium sized lures. When travelling this section of the river a depth sounder is necessary as it helps you to find the deeper water.

There are very few boat launching places for 20 kilometres. Smaller craft can be manhandled down the bank. Within Victoria there is some private land that has no river access unless permission is granted, but camping is not permitted.

This section of the river is very shallow, so take care not to inflict costly damage on your outboard. With only a few deep holes and gutters there are still many native fish holding places among the fallen timber, rock piles or ledges. These are ideal for baitfishing or for trying out your spinnerbaits or small hardbody lures.

Murrabit is a little country town with minimum resources.

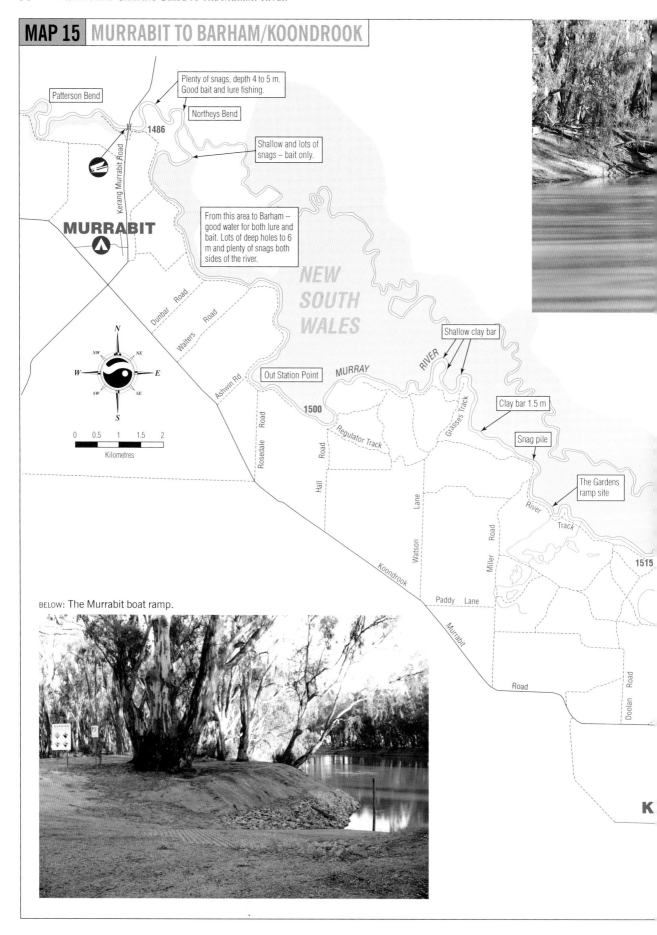

MAP 15 MURRABIT TO BARHAM/KOONDROOK

Patterson Bend

Plenty of snags, depth 4 to 5 m. Good bait and lure fishing.

Northeys Bend

1486

Shallow and lots of snags – bait only.

Kerang Murrabit Road

MURRABIT

From this area to Barham – good water for both lure and bait. Lots of deep holes to 6 m and plenty of snags both sides of the river.

NEW SOUTH WALES

Dunbar Road

Walters Road

N
NW NE
W E
SW SE
S

Ashwin Rd

Out Station Point

MURRAY RIVER

Shallow clay bar

Grasses Track

Clay bar 1.5 m

1500

Regulator Track

Snag pile

0 0.5 1 1.5 2
Kilometres

Rosedale Road

Hall Road

Lane

The Gardens ramp site

River

Track

1515

Watson Lane

Miller Road

Koondrook

Paddy Lane

Murrabit

Road

Doolan Road

BELOW: The Murrabit boat ramp.

K

LEFT: The Little Murray River.

BELOW: Barham road bridge.

NEW SOUTH WALES

MURRAY RIVER

BARHAM

Shallow patches near Barham. Good bait fishing around caravan park on Victorian side. Good cray fishing under bridge.

ROOK

McKenzie Bend

Gunbower Creek

1526

Clump Bend

Shallow bar

Chinaman Bend

Sovereign Bend

MURRABIT TO BARHAM/KOONDROOK

The Little Murray River, which was started at the 1515 marker near Barham, rejoins the Murray River approximately two kilometres upstream of the Murrabit Bridge at 1488. Some of the river in this section has some deep gutters and is ideal for trolling and baitfishing. A depth sounder is necessary when travelling the river to find these gutters and holes. The river between Murrabit and Barham is only about 40 kilometres long and meanders through some very beautiful country.

Boat ramps are rare but we do have a good one in Barham behind the club. Just upstream of the Koondrook sawmill is the Gunbower Creek outlet to the Murray and I have caught many good fish in this area.

LITTLE MURRAY RIVER
(MARRABOOR RIVER)

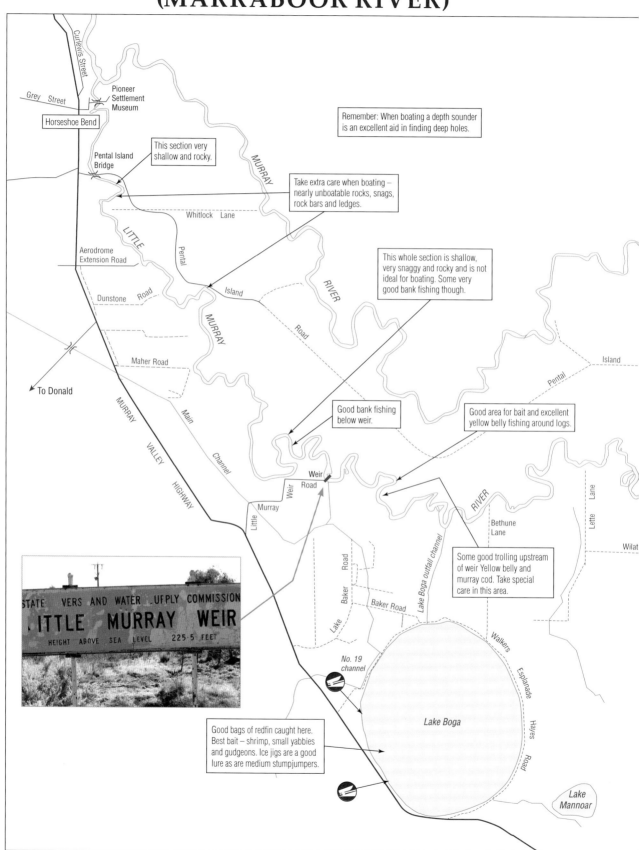

Curlewis Street

Grey   Street

Pioneer
Settlement
Museum

Horseshoe Bend

This section very
shallow and rocky.

Pental Island
Bridge

MURRAY

Remember: When boating a depth sounder
is an excellent aid in finding deep holes.

Take extra care when boating —
nearly unboatable rocks, snags,
rock bars and ledges.

Whitlock   Lane

LITTLE

Aerodrome
Extension Road

Pental

This whole section is shallow,
very snaggy and rocky and is not
ideal for boating. Some very
good bank fishing though.

RIVER

Dunstone   Road

Island

Road

MURRAY

Maher Road

Island

→ To Donald

Pental

MURRAY   VALLEY   HIGHWAY

Main

Channel

Good bank fishing
below weir.

Good area for bait and excellent
yellow belly fishing around logs.

Weir
Road

Weir

RIVER

Little

Murray

Lette Lane

Lette Lane

Bethune
Lane

Wilat

Some good trolling upstream
of weir Yellow belly and
murray cod. Take special
care in this area.

Lake Boga outfall channel

Baker   Road

Baker Road

Lake

Walkers

Esplanade

Hayes   Road

No. 19
channel

Lake Boga

Good bags of redfin caught here.
Best bait — shrimp, small yabbies
and gudgeons. Ice jigs are a good
lure as are medium stumpjumpers.

Lake
Mannoar

LITTLE MURRAY RIVER

There is excellent fishing at the junction of the Pental Island and the Benjeroop Weir. There is also good fishing from the junction of the Loddon River to Fish Point Weir. Most fishing is done from the bank as the little Murray is mostly snags and very shallow.

From Fish Point and Davies road bridge downstream for about half a kilometre is ideal for bait and lure fishing. Boats can be launched here but you need to manhandle then down the bank—so light aluminium boats with small motors are the norm.

Downstream between Vains Road and Lette Lane have produced some good catches at times but be very careful if boating because of rocks and logs.

Some trolling can be done upstream in the weir pool with small lures. From below the weir through to the Murray River the water is shallow and very snaggy, so bank fishing is the way to go.

Little Murray River

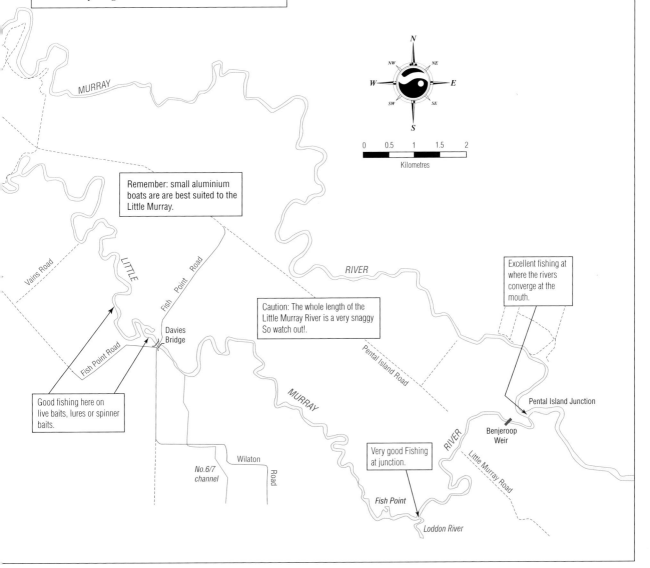

MURRAY

N
NW NE
W E
SW SE
S

0   0.5   1   1.5   2
Kilometres

Remember: small aluminium boats are are best suited to the Little Murray.

RIVER

Excellent fishing at where the rivers converge at the mouth.

Vains Road

LITTLE

Fish Point Road

Davies Bridge

Caution: The whole length of the Little Murray River is a very snaggy So watch out!.

Pental Island Road

Fish Point Road

Good fishing here on live baits, lures or spinner baits.

MURRAY

Pental Island Junction

Benjeroop Weir

RIVER

Little Murray Road

Wilaton Road

No.6/7 channel

Very good Fishing at junction.

Fish Point

Loddon River

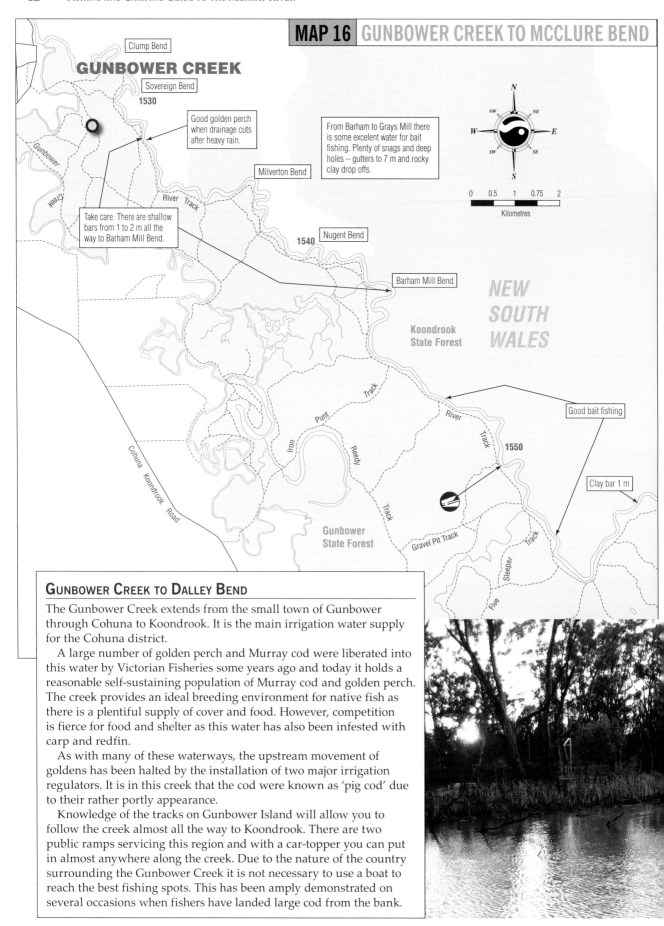

MAP 16 GUNBOWER CREEK TO MCCLURE BEND

Clump Bend

GUNBOWER CREEK

Sovereign Bend

1530

Good golden perch when drainage cuts after heavy rain.

From Barham to Grays Mill there is some excelent water for bait fishing. Plenty of snags and deep holes – gutters to 7 m and rocky clay drop offs.

Milverton Bend

Take care. There are shallow bars from 1 to 2 m all the way to Barham Mill Bend.

River Track

1540 Nugent Bend

Barham Mill Bend

Koondrook State Forest

NEW SOUTH WALES

Good bait fishing

Punt

Iron

Reedy

Track

River

Track

1550

Clay bar 1 m

Cohuna Koondrook Road

Gunbower State Forest

Gravel Pit Track

Sleeper Track

Five

0   0.5   1   0.75   2
Kilometres

GUNBOWER CREEK TO DALLEY BEND

The Gunbower Creek extends from the small town of Gunbower through Cohuna to Koondrook. It is the main irrigation water supply for the Cohuna district.

A large number of golden perch and Murray cod were liberated into this water by Victorian Fisheries some years ago and today it holds a reasonable self-sustaining population of Murray cod and golden perch. The creek provides an ideal breeding environment for native fish as there is a plentiful supply of cover and food. However, competition is fierce for food and shelter as this water has also been infested with carp and redfin.

As with many of these waterways, the upstream movement of goldens has been halted by the installation of two major irrigation regulators. It is in this creek that the cod were known as 'pig cod' due to their rather portly appearance.

Knowledge of the tracks on Gunbower Island will allow you to follow the creek almost all the way to Koondrook. There are two public ramps servicing this region and with a car-topper you can put in almost anywhere along the creek. Due to the nature of the country surrounding the Gunbower Creek it is not necessary to use a boat to reach the best fishing spots. This has been amply demonstrated on several occasions when fishers have landed large cod from the bank.

MAP 16 A MCCLURE BEND TO DALLEY BEND

McClure Bend

McClure Bend has excellent bait fishing. Lure fishing good in and along channel. Also good cray fishing areas.

Logs under water 1.4 m

Cemetery Bend

Good for bait fishing and lures. Also excellent cray fishing during season around clay banks.

Uneven bottom

Nursery Bend

River Track

1560

Rock 1.3 – 2 m

Social Bend

Deep hole near clay ledges. A fishfinder is helpful to locate ledges.

Koondrook State Forest

86 Bend

River

Track

1580

NEW SOUTH WALES

84 Bend

From 84 Bend to Gravel Bend has many fish holding snags and deep water for lures and bait fishing.

Some shallow water 1.2 to 1.8 m

82 Bend

Grand Bend

Gunbower State Forest

Gravel Bend

Good bait fishing towards evening

Sandbar Bend

Stanton Break

Snags 1.8 m under water.

Halfway Bend

Scotty Bend

Some deep holes – mainly bait fishing.

Plenty of snags.

Bonneman Bend

BELOW: Gunbower Creek outfall

Centre channel

This bend has produced some big fish mainly on bait, but lures are worth a run.

Excellent deep water clay ledges. Lower boats on rope.

Kate Malone Bend

Mopoke Bend

1610

Below Torrumbarry the deep water is on the outside of the bends in the river. All have plenty of snags and lures are good. Also an excellent bait fish area.

Long Bend

DALLEY BEND   Dalley Bend

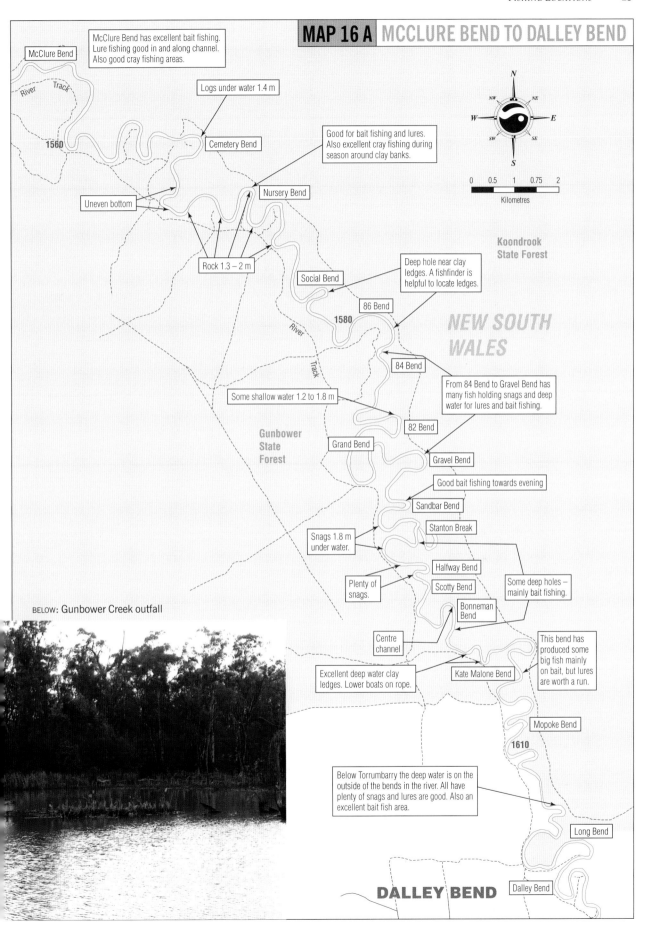

N
NW NE
W E
SW SE
S

0   0.5   1   0.75   2
Kilometres

ABOVE: Torrumbarry Weir Pool

BELOW: Ashley Hinson trolling the Torrumbarry Weir pool.

Torrumbarry Weir

Kow Swamp at sunset.

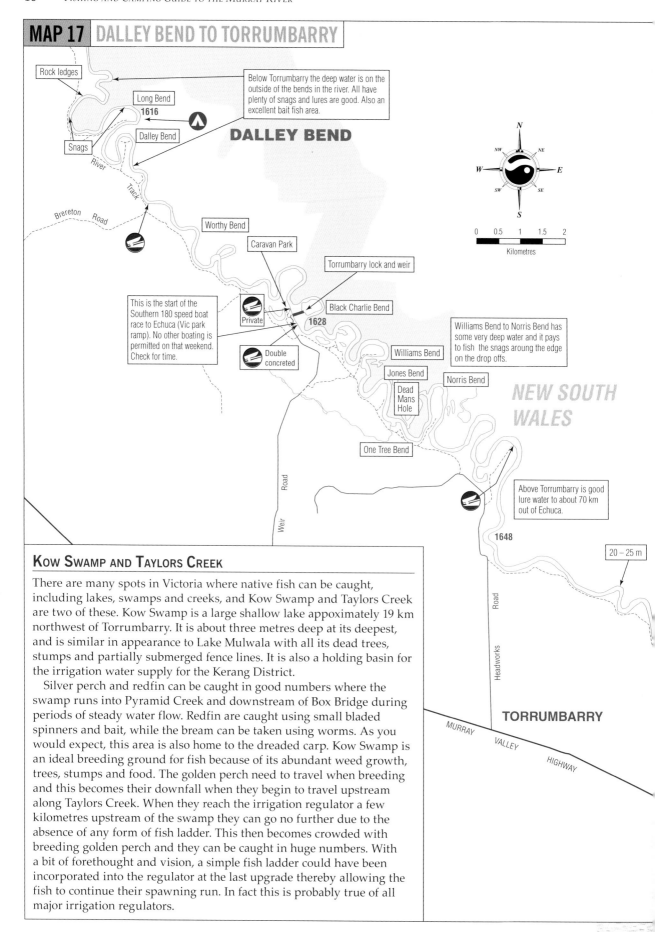

MAP 17 DALLEY BEND TO TORRUMBARRY

Rock ledges

Below Torrumbarry the deep water is on the outside of the bends in the river. All have plenty of snags and lures are good. Also an excellent bait fish area.

Long Bend

1616

Dalley Bend

DALLEY BEND

Snags

River

Track

Brereton Road

Worthy Bend

Caravan Park

Torrumbarry lock and weir

This is the start of the Southern 180 speed boat race to Echuca (Vic park ramp). No other boating is permitted on that weekend. Check for time.

Private

Black Charlie Bend

1628

Double concreted

Williams Bend to Norris Bend has some very deep water and it pays to fish the snags around the edge on the drop offs.

Williams Bend

Jones Bend

Dead Mans Hole

Norris Bend

NEW SOUTH WALES

One Tree Bend

Above Torrumbarry is good lure water to about 70 km out of Echuca.

1648

20 – 25 m

Road

Weir

Road

Headworks Road

TORRUMBARRY

MURRAY VALLEY HIGHWAY

0   0.5   1   1.5   2
Kilometres

KOW SWAMP AND TAYLORS CREEK

There are many spots in Victoria where native fish can be caught, including lakes, swamps and creeks, and Kow Swamp and Taylors Creek are two of these. Kow Swamp is a large shallow lake appoximately 19 km northwest of Torrumbarry. It is about three metres deep at its deepest, and is similar in appearance to Lake Mulwala with all its dead trees, stumps and partially submerged fence lines. It is also a holding basin for the irrigation water supply for the Kerang District.

Silver perch and redfin can be caught in good numbers where the swamp runs into Pyramid Creek and downstream of Box Bridge during periods of steady water flow. Redfin are caught using small bladed spinners and bait, while the bream can be taken using worms. As you would expect, this area is also home to the dreaded carp. Kow Swamp is an ideal breeding ground for fish because of its abundant weed growth, trees, stumps and food. The golden perch need to travel when breeding and this becomes their downfall when they begin to travel upstream along Taylors Creek. When they reach the irrigation regulator a few kilometres upstream of the swamp they can go no further due to the absence of any form of fish ladder. This then becomes crowded with breeding golden perch and they can be caught in huge numbers. With a bit of forethought and vision, a simple fish ladder could have been incorporated into the regulator at the last upgrade thereby allowing the fish to continue their spawning run. In fact this is probably true of all major irrigation regulators.

MAP 17 A TORRUMBARRY TO MOAMA STATE FOREST

20 – 25 m

1656

Bait and lure fishing excellent all the way to Torrumbarry. Plenty of snags and clay banks. Depth averages 4 – 5 m. Speed boat haven during summer time from Torrumbarry to Echuca. Fine if lure fishing at this time.

Deep Creek Marina Houseboats. Good water upstream bait fishing.

NEW SOUTH WALES

Young Road

Bailieu Road

Gravel

1670

MURRAY VALLEY HIGHWAY

Fraser Road

Farley Road

Sand

Timber

Sand

Wills Bend

20 m deep

Bait and lure fishing excellent. Plenty of snags and clay banks. Depth averages 4 – 5 m. Speed boat haven during summer time from Torrumbarry to Echuca. Fine if lure fishing at this time.

1684

MOAMA STATE FOREST

Bait and lure fishing excellent. Plenty of snags and clay banks. Depth averages 4 – 5 m. Speed boat haven during summer time from Torrumbarry to Echuca. Fine if lure fishing at this time.

Concrete

Rock

River Road

Track

O'Sullivan Road

Road

Odwyer Road

Casey Road

Concrete

Planta Road

1698

Concrete private

0   0.5   1   1.5   2
Kilometres

DALLEY BEND TO MOAMA STATE FOREST

The river between Gunbower outfall and Dalley Bend is about 60 kilometres long and winds it way through the Gunbower Island State Forest. This section has plenty of snags and fishy areas, so don't be put off by the shallowness of the water. Excellent fishing can be had in Nursery Bend, bends 86, 84, 82 and Kate Malone's Bend. Cemetery Bend is another renowned cod fishing spot. In fact, there are many deep holes along this section and they all produce good fish throughout the year.

The Gunbower Island State Forest runs parallel to this part of the river. If you are venturing out that way in winter or in inclement weather expect to become bogged unless you are driving a 4WD vehicle. At the other extreme, the summer and dry weather brings rolling clouds of dust that cover anything and everything. I strongly advise you to seek local knowledge and a current map of the area as there is a myriad of tracks throughout the forest and you could easily become lost.

Boat ramps are scarce in this section, we have only one at the Yarrum Cut (wire fence) north of Cohuna. At all other places, boats and equipment need to be manhandled down the bank.

BELOW: Upstream from Torrumbarry.

MOAMA STATE FOREST TO BARMAH

We have a few ramps in this section of river but most of them are private. Vic Park would have to be the pick with the Echuca East ramp ordinary since being extended (not enough slope now). Both have plenty of car parking.

Just on the outskirts of Echuca the Campaspe and Murray rivers join. In winter excellent redfin fishing can be had in the lower reaches of the Campaspe River. Arm yourself with a light rod, reel and some bladed spinners or small plug type lures such as number 3 StumpJumpers and you should be able to score yourself a good feed of fish in short order.

You are now starting to reach that part of the river used by many paddle steamers and houseboats From the historic port of Echuca. It has been said that is why many of the snags have been removed from this stretch of the river. Even if this were true there are still plenty around with lots of good fish to be caught.

Just upstream of the Echuca East boat ramp between the 1718 and 1726 distance markers there are a lot of deep holes, snags, ledges and drop-offs where outstanding fishing can be had.

Further upstream is the junction of the Goulburn River and you can see where the discoloured Goulburn water meets the Murray. Many good fish have been taken on the edge of the discoloured Goulburn water. Access to the river in this area can be gained from Stewarts Bridge Road right through to Barmah or from some of the sand bar boat ramps, but you need to be careful.

At Barmah, boats can be launched under the road bridge at the old vehicular ferry crossing or at the dirt ramp just past the hotel.

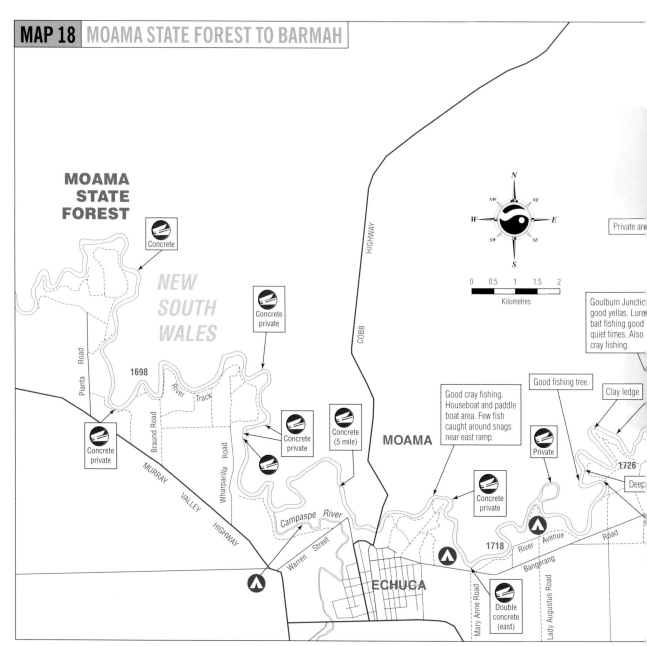

MAP 18 MOAMA STATE FOREST TO BARMAH

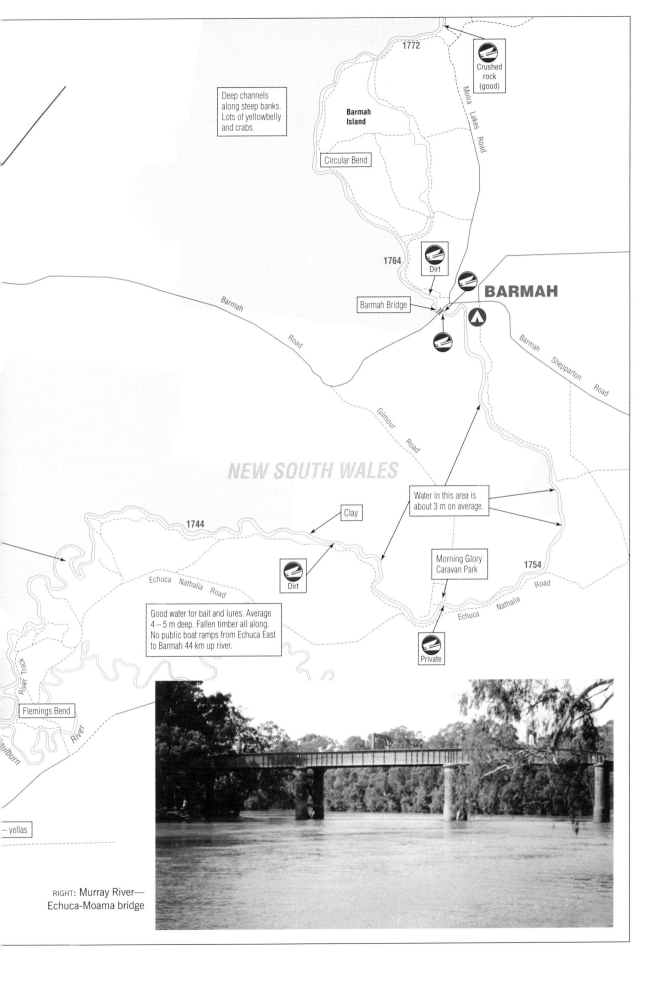

1772

Crushed
rock
(good)

Deep channels
along steep banks.
Lots of yellowbelly
and crabs.

**Barmah
Island**

Moira Lakes Road

Circular Bend

1764

Dirt

BARMAH

Barmah Bridge

Barmah Road

Barmah Shepparton Road

Gilmour Road

NEW SOUTH WALES

Water in this area is
about 3 m on average.

Clay

1744

Morning Glory
Caravan Park

1754

Echuca Nathalia Road

Dirt

Echuca Nathalia Road

Good water for bait and lures. Average
4 – 5 m deep. Fallen timber all along.
No public boat ramps from Echuca East
to Barmah 44 km up river.

Private

River Track

Flemings Bend

River

oulburn

– yellas

RIGHT: Murray River—
Echuca-Moama bridge

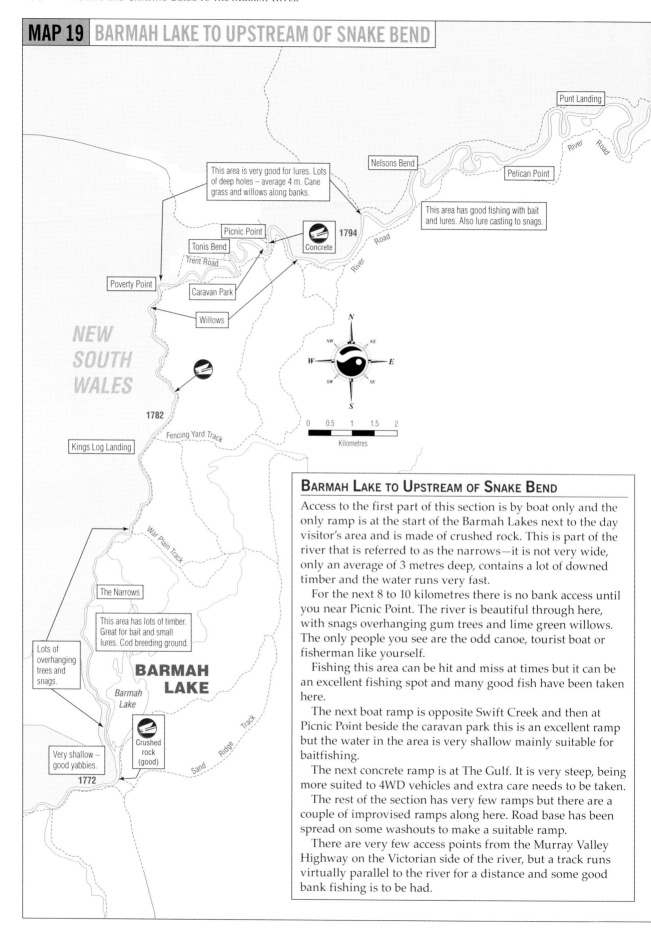

MAP 19 BARMAH LAKE TO UPSTREAM OF SNAKE BEND

Punt Landing

Nelsons Bend

Pelican Point

River Road

This area is very good for lures. Lots of deep holes – average 4 m. Cane grass and willows along banks.

This area has good fishing with bait and lures. Also lure casting to snags.

Picnic Point

1794

Concrete

Tonis Bend

Trent Road

Poverty Point

Caravan Park

Willows

NEW SOUTH WALES

N
NW NE
W E
SW SE
S

0   0.5   1   1.5   2
Kilometres

1782

Fencing Yard Track

Kings Log Landing

War Plain Track

The Narrows

This area has lots of timber. Great for bait and small lures. Cod breeding ground.

Lots of overhanging trees and snags.

BARMAH LAKE

Barmah Lake

Crushed rock (good)

Very shallow – good yabbies.

1772

Sand Ridge Track

BARMAH LAKE TO UPSTREAM OF SNAKE BEND

Access to the first part of this section is by boat only and the only ramp is at the start of the Barmah Lakes next to the day visitor's area and is made of crushed rock. This is part of the river that is referred to as the narrows—it is not very wide, only an average of 3 metres deep, contains a lot of downed timber and the water runs very fast.

For the next 8 to 10 kilometres there is no bank access until you near Picnic Point. The river is beautiful through here, with snags overhanging gum trees and lime green willows. The only people you see are the odd canoe, tourist boat or fisherman like yourself.

Fishing this area can be hit and miss at times but it can be an excellent fishing spot and many good fish have been taken here.

The next boat ramp is opposite Swift Creek and then at Picnic Point beside the caravan park this is an excellent ramp but the water in the area is very shallow mainly suitable for baitfishing.

The next concrete ramp is at The Gulf. It is very steep, being more suited to 4WD vehicles and extra care needs to be taken.

The rest of the section has very few ramps but there are a couple of improvised ramps along here. Road base has been spread on some washouts to make a suitable ramp.

There are very few access points from the Murray Valley Highway on the Victorian side of the river, but a track runs virtually parallel to the river for a distance and some good bank fishing is to be had.

LEFT: Patrick Hunt and Bruce Collins with a Murray cod caught in The Narrows near Barmah using a bardi grub.

BELOW: Ron Robinson with a good size Murray cod caught on an Outlaw Spinnerbait.

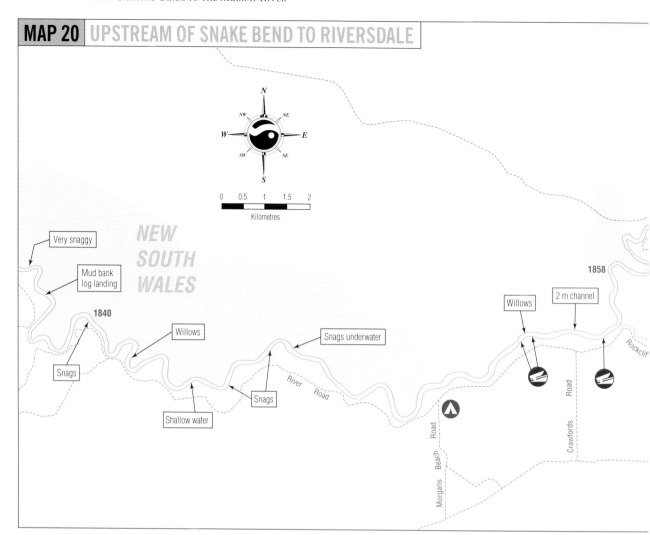

MAP 20 | UPSTREAM OF SNAKE BEND TO RIVERSDALE

NEW SOUTH WALES

Very snaggy

Mud bank log landing

1840

Snags

Willows

Shallow water

Snags

River Road

Snags underwater

1858

Willows

2 m channel

Rockclif

Road

Crawfords Road

Morgans Beach Road

0 0.5 1 1.5 2
Kilometres

ABOVE: Flooded Red River Gums

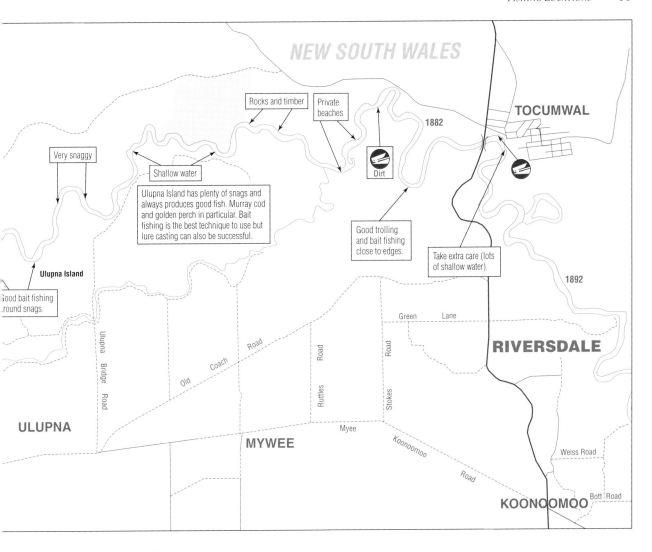

UPSTREAM OF SNAKE BEND TO RIVERSDALE

As we move upstream some stretches of the river are very wide in places and it seems to have fewer snags in it than other parts. However, these snags are outstanding fishing spots and I recommend that they should be explored extensively. The beaches along here are not as prominent as in other areas but boast many good drop-offs and ledges. The water gives the appearance of not moving as quickly here and this may be due to the river's width and depth.

There are a few boat ramps in this section and I would have no hesitation in launching our five metre craft anywhere along here. Ulupna Island is a very popular place with the locals, as well as tourists, for fishing and camping, and the camping area fills quickly during holidays.

RIGHT: Redfin make excellent eating, and this one is definitely headed for a plate!

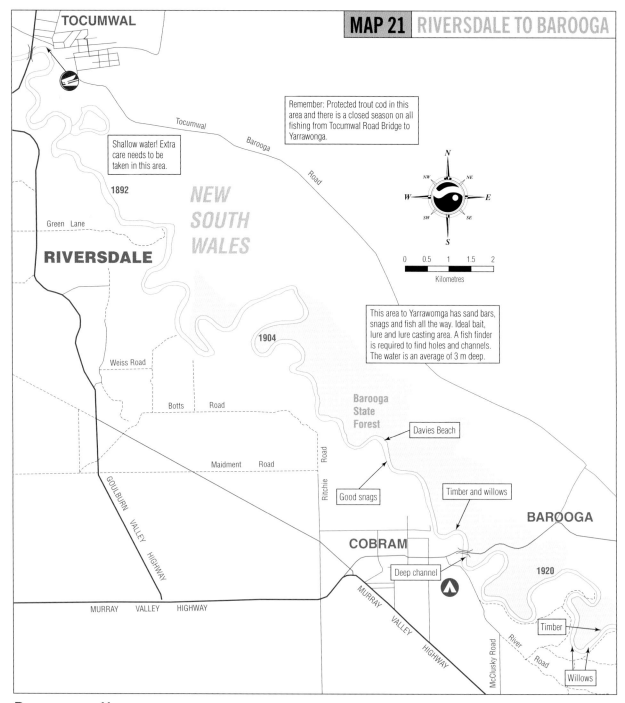

MAP 21 RIVERSDALE TO BAROOGA

TOCUMWAL

Shallow water! Extra care needs to be taken in this area.

1892

Green Lane

RIVERSDALE

NEW SOUTH WALES

Tocumwal

Barooga

Road

Remember: Protected trout cod in this area and there is a closed season on all fishing from Tocumwal Road Bridge to Yarrawonga.

This area to Yarrawomga has sand bars, snags and fish all the way. Ideal bait, lure and lure casting area. A fish finder is required to find holes and channels. The water is an average of 3 m deep.

0   0.5   1   1.5   2
Kilometres

Weiss Road

1904

Botts   Road

Maidment   Road

Barooga State Forest

Davies Beach

Ritchie   Road

Good snags

Timber and willows

BAROOGA

GOULBURN VALLEY HIGHWAY

COBRAM

Deep channel

1920

MURRAY   VALLEY   HIGHWAY

MURRAY VALLEY HIGHWAY

McClusky Road

River   Road

Timber

Willows

RIVERSDALE TO YARRAMUNDEE

This area of river between Riversdale and Yarramundee has many beautiful sandy beaches, sand bars and excellent camping sites in the forest areas lining the river. Obviously it is extremely popular during holiday time and can get quite crowded.

Many access points are available from side roads running off the Murray Valley Highway. These join with tracks that wind through the red gum forests to the river. There are a number of boat ramps—some cut into the bank—and boats can also be launched from certain sandbars. You need to exercise great care when using these launching sites as your car or vehicle may become bogged very quickly. A word of warning—

seasonal low water can expose normally submerged mud banks and timber. The water can become dangerously shallow and you need to be very careful when boating at these times.

This section of river boasts a number of excellent concrete boat ramps. These can be found on the town beach in Tocumwal, at Thompson's Beach (close to the town water supply) in Cobram and Horseshoe Lagoon.

The river between Yarrawonga and the Tocumwal Road Bridge is the location of one of the only self-sustaining populations of trout cod in Australia. This reach of the river has its own special fishing regulations and closed season.

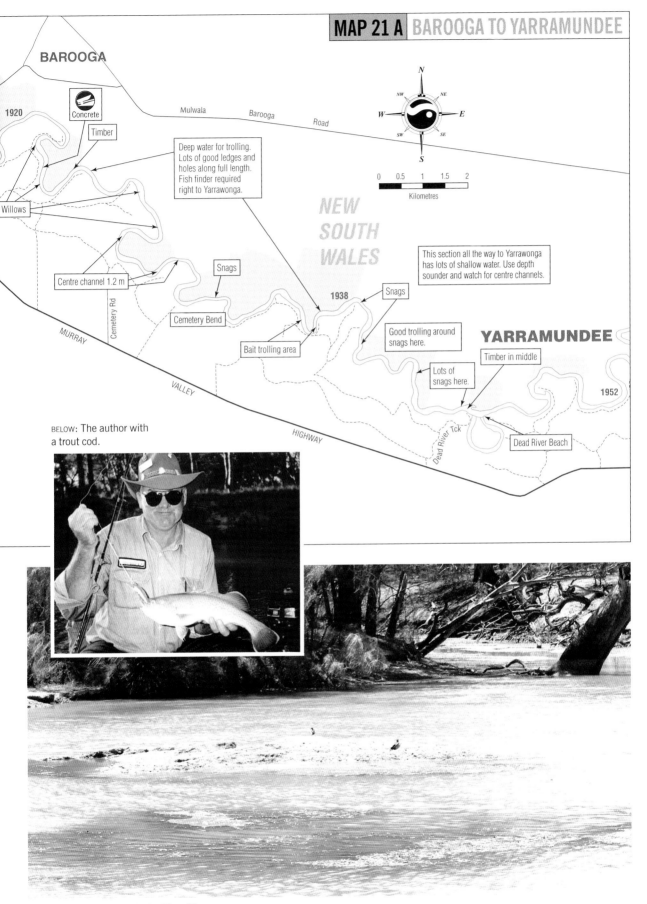

MAP 21 A BAROOGA TO YARRAMUNDEE

BAROOGA

1920

Concrete

Timber

Mulwala — Barooga — Road

N
NW *NE*
W *E*
SW *SE*
S

0   0.5   1   1.5   2
Kilometres

NEW SOUTH WALES

Willows

Deep water for trolling. Lots of good ledges and holes along full length. Fish finder required right to Yarrawonga.

Centre channel 1.2 m

Snags

Cemetery Bend

Cemetery Rd

MURRAY

This section all the way to Yarrawonga has lots of shallow water. Use depth sounder and watch for centre channels.

1938

Snags

Good trolling around snags here.

YARRAMUNDEE

Bait trolling area

Lots of snags here.

Timber in middle

1952

VALLEY

HIGHWAY

Dead River Tck

Dead River Beach

BELOW: The author with a trout cod.

ABOVE: A typical sand bar in the River Murray.

ABOVE: Bill Blacksell with his Murray cod caught on a StumpJumper lure.

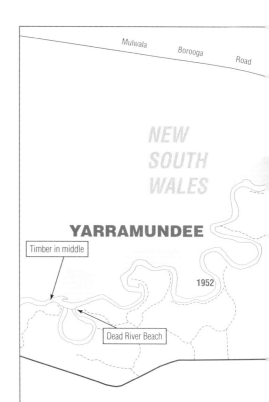

Mulwala   Borooga   Road

NEW SOUTH WALES

YARRAMUNDEE

Timber in middle

1952

Dead River Beach

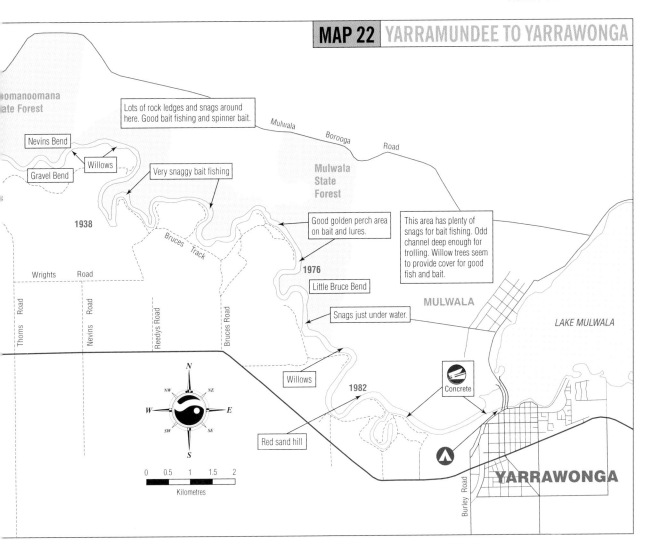

MAP 22 YARRAMUNDEE TO YARRAWONGA

Lots of rock ledges and snags around here. Good bait fishing and spinner bait.

Nevins Bend

Willows

Gravel Bend

1938

Bruces Track

Wrights Road

Thoms Road

Nevins Road

Reedys Road

Bruces Road

Very snaggy bait fishing

Mulwala Borooga Road

Mulwala State Forest

Good golden perch area on bait and lures.

1976

Little Bruce Bend

This area has plenty of snags for bait fishing. Odd channel deep enough for trolling. Willow trees seem to provide cover for good fish and bait.

MULWALA

LAKE MULWALA

Snags just under water.

Willows

1982

Concrete

Red sand hill

YARRAWONGA

Burley Road

N NW NE W E SW SE S

0 0.5 1 1.5 2
Kilometres

ABOVE: Also caught on a StumpJumper lure!

YARRAMUNDEE TO YARRAWONGA

This section of river has everything that a fisherman or holiday camper could require. Sandbars are very popular during the holiday period and make good camping areas, so you need to obtain your spots early. Many access points to the river are available from side roads into the forest running off the Murray Valley Highway. Some places have a river road that travels a distance beside the picturesque river. When boating this area you need to take extra care because of the many sandbars, snags and very shallow water at times. There are many good fish holding snags for both bait, lures and spinnerbaits fisherman that should not overlooked.

Yarrawonga is situated on the shores of Lake Mulwala. We will not talk about Lake Mulwala but about the river downstream of the dam wall. First point of entry at Yarrawonga is downstream of the weir at the Caravan Park. An expansive park, it boasts two ramps, however only one can be used to launch boats from a trailer. The other is out of the water during the normal season. The public ramps can be accessed from the road that runs adjacent to the Caravan Park's administration offices. The water moves quickly through this area and at certain times of the year golden perch may congregate below the weir wall and good catches can be made. This section is home to the only self-sustaining population of trout cod in Australia and is subject to its own fishing regulations and closed season.

MAP 23 YARRAWONGA TO COLLENDINA STATE FOREST

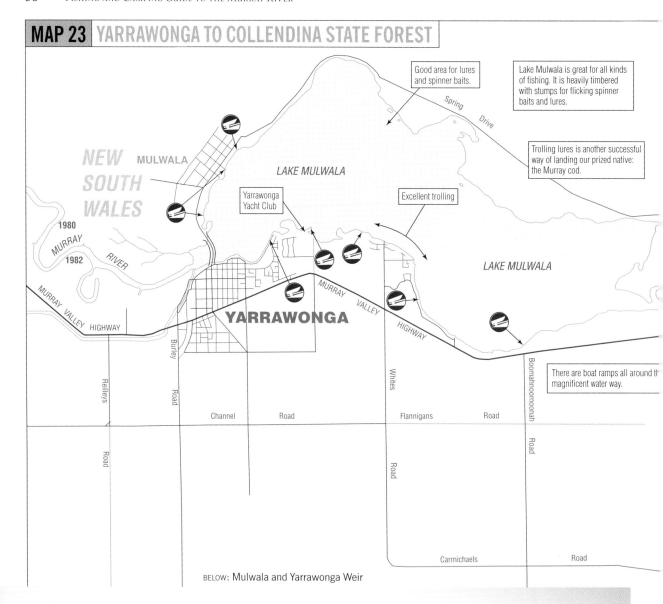

Good area for lures and spinner baits.

Lake Mulwala is great for all kinds of fishing. It is heavily timbered with stumps for flicking spinner baits and lures.

NEW SOUTH WALES

MULWALA

LAKE MULWALA

Trolling lures is another successful way of landing our prized native: the Murray cod.

Yarrawonga Yacht Club

Excellent trolling

1980

MURRAY

1982

RIVER

LAKE MULWALA

YARRAWONGA

MURRAY VALLEY HIGHWAY

MURRAY VALLEY HIGHWAY

Spring   Drive

There are boat ramps all around the magnificent water way.

Reilleys   Road

Burley   Road

Channel   Road

Whites   Road

Flannigans   Road

Boomahnoomoonah   Road

Carmichaels   Road

BELOW: Mulwala and Yarrawonga Weir

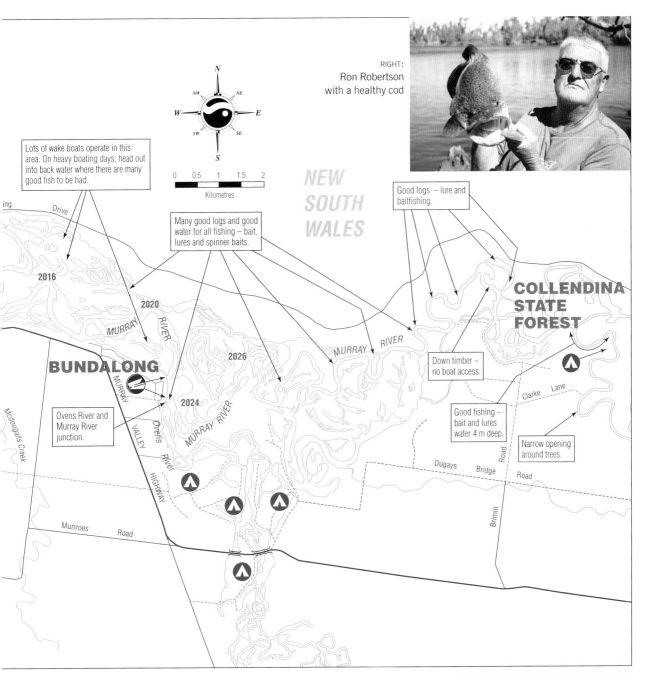

RIGHT:
Ron Robertson
with a healthy cod

Lots of wake boats operate in this area. On heavy boating days, head out into back water where there are many good fish to be had.

NEW SOUTH WALES

Good logs – lure and baitfishing.

Many good logs and good water for all fishing – bait, lures and spinner baits.

2016

2020

MURRAY RIVER

2026

BUNDALONG

COLLENDINA STATE FOREST

MURRAY RIVER

Down timber – no boat access.

Clarke Lane

Ovens River and Murray River junction.

2024

MURRAY RIVER

OVENS RIVER VALLEY HIGHWAY

Good fishing – bait and lures water 4 m deep.

Narrow opening around trees.

Dugays Bridge Road

Brimin Road

Mcdougalls Creek

Munroes   Road

Yarrawonga to Collendina State Forest

The Victorian side of Lake Mulwala provides some of the best boating facilities of the area. There are boat ramps at the Yarrawonga Yacht Club, the bottom of Wood Wood Road and off the River Road. Only limited parking is available at the River Road boat ramp. Fishing out in the tree stumps and trolling lures have produced some excellent fish.

The New South Wales side of this picturesque lake has plenty of camping within the township of Mulwala with excellent boating and picnic facilities as well. Kuffins Reserve, not far out of Mulwala, provides great camping and a good boat ramp. There are some awesome trees plus logs to flick lures around. Many fishermen have caught their personal best cod from this area.

ABOVE: Author Brian Hinson with a Murray cod prior to release.

LEFT: Campsite on Mulwala Island

RIGHT: Yarrawonga Weir – there is no boat access through weir

BELOW: Sunset across Lake Mulwala taken from the campsite on Mulwala Island

Excellent fishing can be had around the edge of channels through the timber on the Victorian side of Lake Mulwala. There are several great boat ramps with camping and picnic areas. The ramp at Hogans is a top spot and has a good picnic area. Fishing around the willows from the bank can be very productive, whilst fishing the timber with Outlaw Spinnerbaits has produced many excellent cod.

The top part of Mulwala around the Everglades, has a couple of islands to camp on, but they are only accessible by boat. Majors Lane provides an excellent boat ramp and has rubbish collection, however no camping is permitted. To access the Everglades by road, you will need to use the Corowa Road on the New South Wales side.

Very good fishing of all types can be had as you pass through the Collendina State Forest. There is great back water at the junction of the Ovens and Murray Rivers near Bundalong. This is one of Brian Hinson's favourite fishing areas. It has excellent boat ramps and picnic facilities. Camping below Bundalong is mainly accessed by boat.

The Ovens River is great to chase native fish, and can be very productive. The lower Ovens has many little creeks that flow during high rainfall. Where these small backwater creeks enter the Ovens, there is an abundance of food, that makes them always worth fishing. There are a couple of good camping sites, with the Lower Ovens Regional Park, Taylors Bend and the end of Clarke Lane being some of the better ones. There is a good boat ramp to access this section at Traveller's Point.

COLLENDINA STATE FOREST TO HOWLONG

Between 2052 to 2062 the river is very shallow – around 0.5 to 1 metre – and covered with timber almost across the narrow river. Just below 2062, the river flows to the right, but there is no boating allowed so you must keep left.

There are some excellent fishing areas in this section with up to 5 metres of water around the willows and cliffs. Take extra care when boating around 2068 as there are large stumps in the middle of the river. Good

LEFT: Camping at Stantons Bend

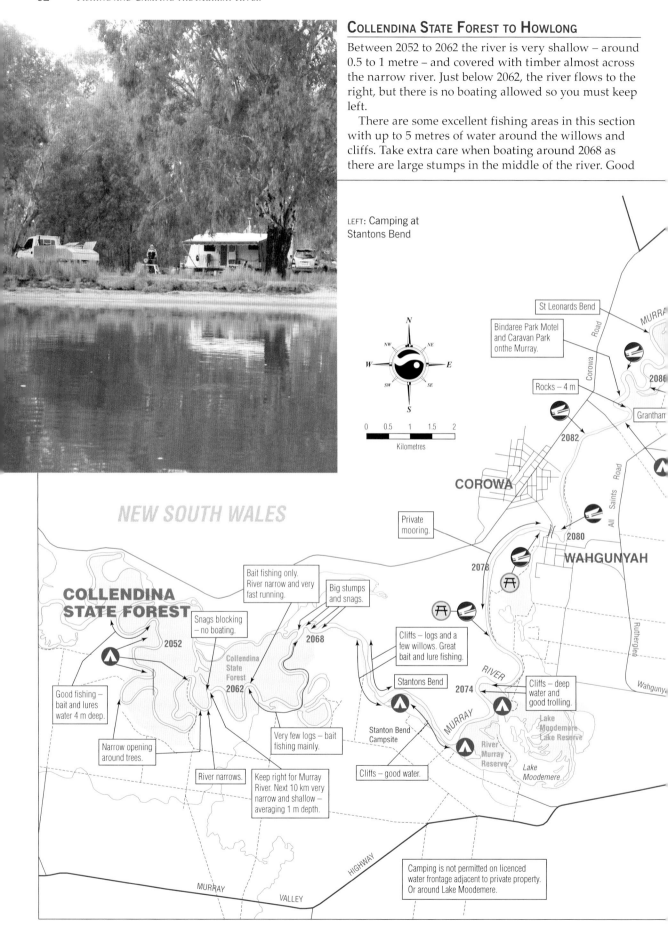

N
NW   NE
W   E
SW   SE
S

0   0.5   1   1.5   2
Kilometres

St Leonards Bend

Bindaree Park Motel and Caravan Park on the Murray.

MURRA

Rocks – 4 m

2086

2082

Grantham

COROWA

Private mooring.

2080

WAHGUNYAH

2078

NEW SOUTH WALES

COLLENDINA STATE FOREST

Bait fishing only. River narrow and very fast running.

Big stumps and snags.

Snags blocking – no boating.

2052

Collendina State Forest

2068

2062

Cliffs – logs and a few willows. Great bait and lure fishing.

Stantons Bend

Cliffs – deep water and good trolling.

2074

RIVER

Wahguny

Good fishing – bait and lures water 4 m deep.

Narrow opening around trees.

Very few logs – bait fishing mainly.

Stanton Bend Campsite

MURRAY

River Murray Reserve

Lake Moodemere Lake Reserve

Lake Moodemere

River narrows.

Keep right for Murray River. Next 10 km very narrow and shallow – averaging 1 m depth.

Cliffs – good water.

Camping is not permitted on licenced water frontage adjacent to private property. Or around Lake Moodemere.

MURRAY   VALLEY   HIGHWAY

camping can be found on the River Murray Reserve and at Lumby Bend.

The next section of the river has many good boat ramps and camping areas. Hoskin Bend and Stanton Bend have excellent camping and picnic facilities as has the Murray Reserve at Lake Moodemere near the walking track. Fishing around the cliff face can provide good fish using Outlaw Spinnerbaits.

There are great camping and picnic areas on both sides of the river at Wahgunyah, Victoria and Corowa,

New South Wales, plus well maintained boat ramps. Fuel is available a short walk down Bridge Road on the Corowa side.

Private boat moorings line the New South Wales side of the river. Casting Outlaw Spinnerbaits will give access to the fish holding up under the boats.

A little further up river from Corowa, the River Murray Reserve provides good camping and bank fishing. There are good casting opportunities around the creek mouths in about 2.5 – 4 metre depths.

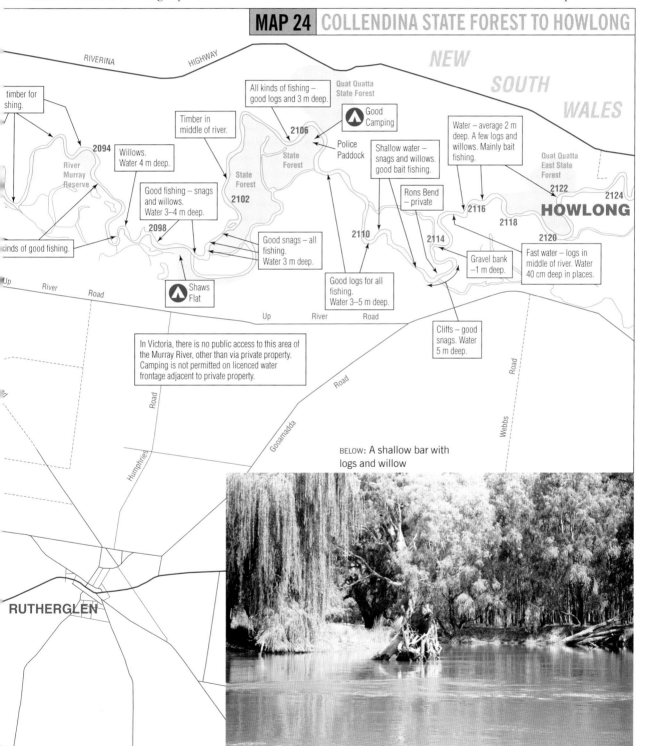

MAP 24 COLLENDINA STATE FOREST TO HOWLONG

RIVERINA HIGHWAY

NEW SOUTH WALES

timber for shing.

All kinds of fishing – good logs and 3 m deep.

Quat Quatta State Forest

Good Camping

2106

Timber in middle of river.

Police Paddock

2094

Willows. Water 4 m deep.

River Murray Reserve

State Forest

State Forest

2102

Shallow water – snags and willows. good bait fishing.

Water – average 2 m deep. A few logs and willows. Mainly bait fishing.

Quat Quatta East State Forest

2122   2124

HOWLONG

2116

Good fishing – snags and willows. Water 3–4 m deep.

2098

Good snags – all fishing. Water 3 m deep.

Rons Bend – private

2118

2120

Fast water – logs in middle of river. Water 40 cm deep in places.

kinds of good fishing.

2110

2114

Gravel bank –1 m deep.

Shaws Flat

Good logs for all fishing. Water 3–5 m deep.

Up   River   Road

Up   River   Road

Cliffs – good snags. Water 5 m deep.

In Victoria, there is no public access to this area of the Murray River, other than via private property. Camping is not permitted on licenced water frontage adjacent to private property.

Road

Road

Webbs   Road

Gooramadda   Road

Humphries

BELOW: A shallow bar with logs and willow

RUTHERGLEN

Bindaree Caravan Park, offering all types of camping, backs on to the river, and has its own boat ramp into excellent water. You can purchase provisions here.

The next section of river has plenty of everything a fisherman might need – except for boat ramps. There are some good logs in 2.5 – 3 metres of water, willows in 3 – 4 metres and some channels around willows in 7 metres ideal for trolling runs.

The New South Wales side of the river has good camping on flat ground with tables etc at the Quat Quatta State Forest and Police Paddock also has good camping. On the Victorian side, the River Murray Reserve and Shaws Flat are best.

Between 2118 and 2122 the water has only a few snags and willows with an average depth of 2 metres, so is better suited to bait fishing.

ABOVE: Lumby Bend camp site.

LEFT: Good bait fishing area.

BELOW: Corowa – Wahgubyah Road Bridge.

ABOVE: Bundaree Bridge

LEFT: River view upstream of Police Paddock

BELOW: Cliffs 4 km downstream of Police Paddock

LEFT: Releasing a good size Murray cod

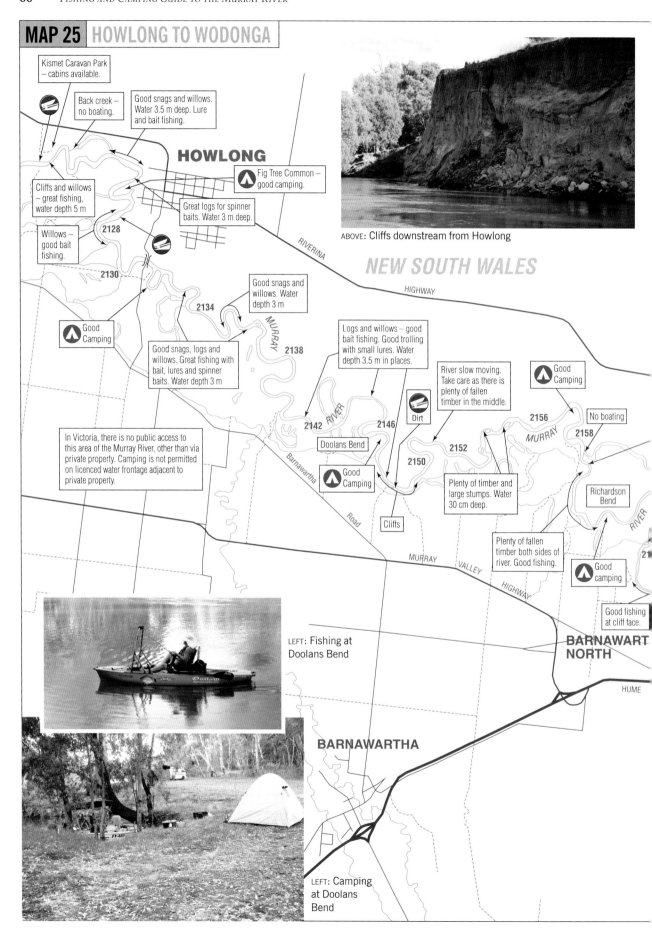

MAP 25 HOWLONG TO WODONGA

Kismet Caravan Park – cabins available.

Back creek – no boating.

Good snags and willows. Water 3.5 m deep. Lure and bait fishing.

HOWLONG

Fig Tree Common – good camping.

Cliffs and willows – great fishing, water depth 5 m

Great logs for spinner baits. Water 3 m deep.

Willows – good bait fishing.

2128

2130

ABOVE: Cliffs downstream from Howlong

RIVERINA

NEW SOUTH WALES

HIGHWAY

Good snags and willows. Water depth 3 m

2134

Good Camping

MURRAY

2138

Good snags, logs and willows. Great fishing with bait, lures and spinner baits. Water depth 3 m

Logs and willows – good bait fishing. Good trolling with small lures. Water depth 3.5 m in places.

River slow moving. Take care as there is plenty of fallen timber in the middle.

Good Camping

2156

No boating

2158

MURRAY

Dirt

2142

RIVER

2146

2152

2150

In Victoria, there is no public access to this area of the Murray River, other than via private property. Camping is not permitted on licenced water frontage adjacent to private property.

Doolans Bend

Good Camping

Barnawartha

Cliffs

Plenty of timber and large stumps. Water 30 cm deep.

Richardson Bend

RIVER

21

Plenty of fallen timber both sides of river. Good fishing.

Good camping

Road

MURRAY

VALLEY

HIGHWAY

Good fishing at cliff face.

BARNAWART NORTH

HUME

LEFT: Fishing at Doolans Bend

BARNAWARTHA

LEFT: Camping at Doolans Bend

HOWLONG TO WODONGA

Kismet Caravan Park backs right on to the river and has its own boat ramp. There are many small creeks flowing into the Murray River in this section, but no boating is permitted. However, there is nothing to stop you from targetting fish at the mouths of these streams, and good fish can be taken here in 4 metres of water.

The next section includes Howlong where you are able to stock up on all provisions. It is a beautiful part of the river with camping and picnic areas. With cliffs, willows and logs in 2 – 6 metres of water it is ideal for lure and bait fishing.

Some good picnic and camping is provided at Doolans Bend and the River Murray Reserve. There is a dirt boat ramp at the cliffs off Stewart Road. Plenty of fishing with lures and bait is to be had around willows, logs and deeper channels between 2134 and 2142. Logs and blue stone have been placed along the river banks to stabilize them.

Good camping can be found on the River Murray Reserve, but very little fishing due to the shallow water. Extra care is needed through the area between 2154 and 2160 as the shallow water (15 cm) has logs and stumps right across the river.

The next section of the Murray River has some very good islands that collect floating timber, making a great target to cast at with bibless and Outlaw Spinnerbaits.

There is good productive fishing to be had around the cliff face in about 4.5 metres of water. The Richards Reserve area offers excellent camping and fishing.

With depths of between 2.5 to 4 metres, with plenty of willows makes for some good fishing through the next section. However, just below the 2178 mark, a rock bar in only 20 to 40 centimetres of water goes right across the river. Take extra care if crossing this bar.

Wonga Wetlands is inundated with a great mixture of wildlife amongst the system of lagoons and billabongs. It is well worthwhile investigating by the photographer or wildlife enthusiast. Just below the Wonga Wetland there are some great casting opportunities for spinnerbaits.

Passing by the Wodonga Regional Park through to the outside of Wodonga, fishing is mainly off the bank. With not many logs for casting, it is best suited for baitfishing.

On the outskirts of Albury, you will come across many parks, such as Padman Park, and Mates Park. These parks are great picnic areas and fishing is mainly from the bank. Wodonga Regional Park is on the Victorian side of the river and there is very little boat launching access.

Snags across river – need to lift motor – water 60 cm deep.

Good camping on island

RIVERINA

Take care – small passage through trees – water depth 30cm –1 m

HIGHWAY

Good fishing – 2 big fallen trees.

Shallow rock bars – extra care needed.

Flat bottom – few willows, some logs. Bait fishing and little flicking lures.

Loop closed to all boating.

2170

Dangerous rock bars – water 45 cm deep.

2178

NEW SOUTH WALES

gs in middle of r. 90 cm deep.

Mud bank

Big log in middle of river.

Plenty of fallen timber in fast flowing water. Mainly bait fishing.

2182

MURRAY

Wonga Wetlands

Good fishing logs.

Mainly bait fishing.

2192

ALBURY

Albury Wodonga Regional Park

FREEWAY

Timber in middle of river. 2 km of 1 m depth.

RIVER

2186

Water 3 m deep. Willows and logs for casting. Good bait fishing.

N
NW NE
W E
SW SE
S

HUME

FREEWAY

0 0.5 1 1.5 2
Kilometres

WODONGA

ABOVE: One of the many areas where efforts have been made to stabilize the Murray River banks.

BELOW: A couple of fishermen enjoying the river at the back of the Kismet Caravan and Cabin Park.

Picturesque Murray River scene at Howling

LEFT: Old Kismet boat ramp

RIGHT: A typical dirt boat ramp

Side stream block to boating

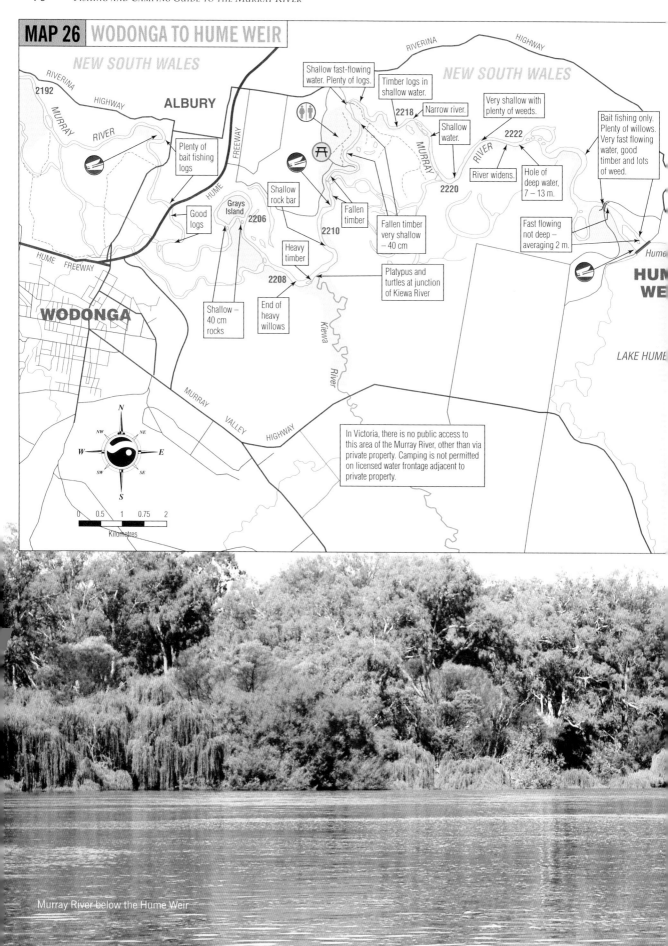

MAP 26 WODONGA TO HUME WEIR

NEW SOUTH WALES

RIVERINA HIGHWAY

NEW SOUTH WALES

2192

MURRAY RIVER

RIVERINA HIGHWAY

ALBURY

FREEWAY

HUME

Shallow fast-flowing water. Plenty of logs.

Timber logs in shallow water.

2218

Narrow river.

Shallow water.

MURRAY RIVER

2220

Very shallow with plenty of weeds.

2222

River widens.

Hole of deep water, 7 – 13 m.

Bait fishing only. Plenty of willows. Very fast flowing water, good timber and lots of weed.

Plenty of bait fishing logs

Good logs

Grays Island

2206

Shallow rock bar

Fallen timber

2210

Fallen timber very shallow – 40 cm

Heavy timber

2208

Shallow – 40 cm rocks

End of heavy willows

Platypus and turtles at junction of Kiewa River

Fast flowing not deep – averaging 2 m.

Hume

HUM
WE

Kiewa River

HUME FREEWAY

WODONGA

MURRAY VALLEY HIGHWAY

LAKE HUME

In Victoria, there is no public access to this area of the Murray River, other than via private property. Camping is not permitted on licensed water frontage adjacent to private property.

N
NW NE
W   E
SW SE
S

0 0.5 1 0.75 2
Kilometres

Murray River below the Hume Weir

ABOVE: Great fish holding area – a major spinner bait workout!

RIGHT: The Hume Weir from the river.

WODONGA TO HUME WEIR

This section of the Murray River now passes through Albury East and South Albury. It has several great picnic areas within town limits and fishing from the banks. Boat ramps are few and far between with one at Hovell Tree Park. On the Victorian side of the river, are parts of the Wodonga Regional Park, and the best fishing is in the mouth of the Wodonga Creek where there is a mixture of rocks and logs.

We now come into a very scenic part of the river with willow lined banks and the Hume Weir in the background. The water here is extremely fast flowing, but has some great backwater with plenty of good fish. The road bridge here has great pylons with fish holding close.

Around this area the backwaters are lined with ribbon weed that attracts fish chasing a feed. Just downstream of the road bridge are the first of the main rock bars where extra care is needed when boating. The only boat ramp found in this section is right at the bottom of Hume Weir and proved to be an excellent all weather ramp.

ABOVE LAKE HUME

LAKE HUME TO JINGELLIC

This area like all in the Upper Murray area is very scenic and offers some great fishing for Murray cod and occasionally trout cod. Please be aware that trout cod are protected and must be released unharmed when captured. (See accompanying diagrams).

There are also plenty of trout in the cooler months, although the trout fishing tends to be more consistent above Towong. The water here is somewhat deeper than the upper reaches but there are still several rapids that can form (depending on the water level and river height at the time). So, if you are on the water in a boat and travelling downstream and encounter a rapid do not run the rapid if you need to back up stream to your launching place.

There is only one dedicated launching ramp in

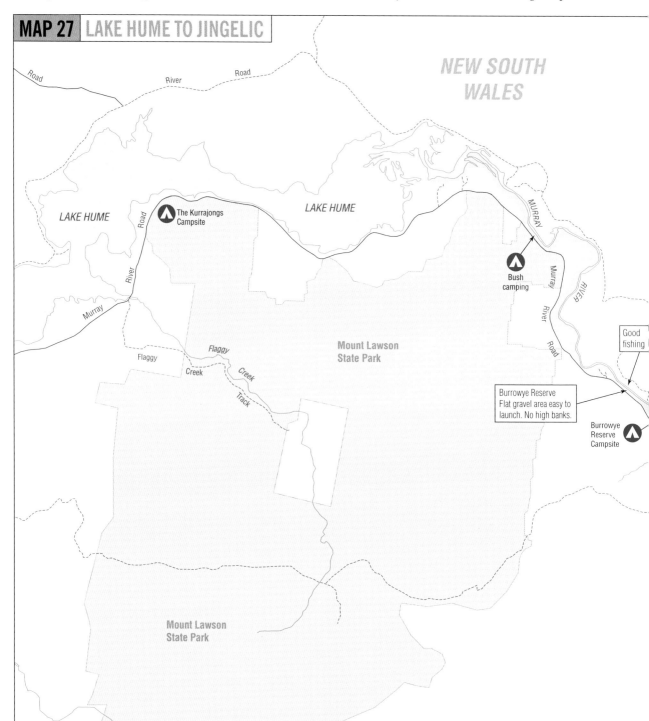

MAP 27 LAKE HUME TO JINGELIC

NEW SOUTH WALES

Road   River   Road

LAKE HUME

The Kurrajongs Campsite

LAKE HUME

MURRAY

Road

River

Murray

Bush camping

Murray   River

Good fishing

Flaggy   Flaggy   Creek

Flaggy   Creek

Track

Mount Lawson State Park

Burrowye Reserve
Flat gravel area easy to launch. No high banks.

Burrowye Reserve Campsite

Mount Lawson State Park

this section, a concrete ramp located at the Jingellic Camping Reserve. The river is generally navigable and relatively deep here however again if the level drops and rapids form, don't proceed if you need to return to the ramp.

Land based access throughout is reasonable and there are a number of designated and bush camping spots in this section. (Refer to accompanying map).

There are several other access points where boats can be launched.

LEFT: Upper Murray cod

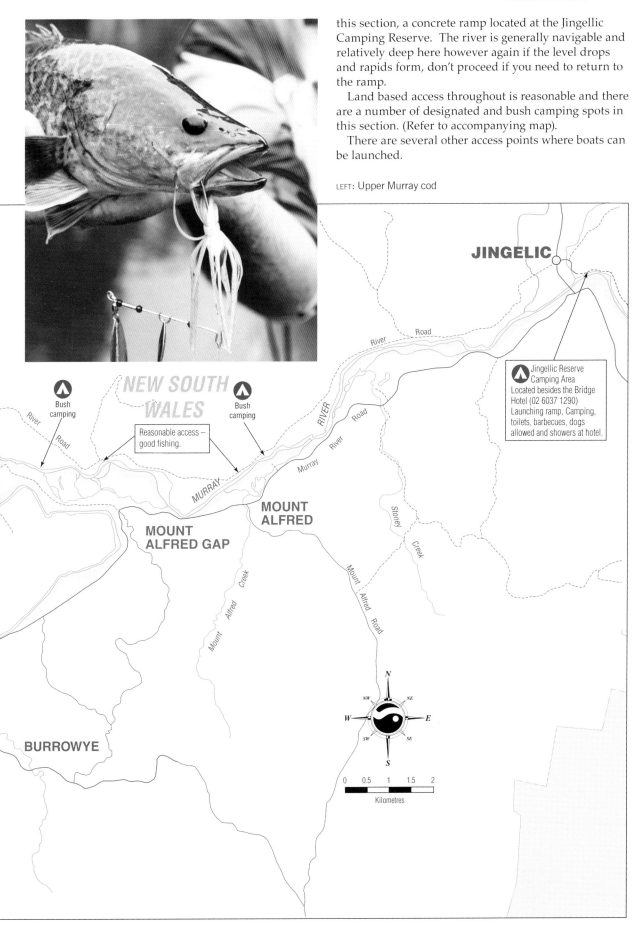

JINGELIC

Jingellic Reserve Camping Area
Located besides the Bridge Hotel (02 6037 1290) Launching ramp, Camping, toilets, barbecues, dogs allowed and showers at hotel.

NEW SOUTH WALES

Bush camping

Bush camping

Reasonable access – good fishing.

MURRAY

RIVER

Murray River

River Road

Road

River Road

Stoney Creek

MOUNT ALFRED

MOUNT ALFRED GAP

Mount Alfred Creek

Mount Alfred Road

BURROWYE

N
NW   NE
W   E
SW   SE
S

0   0.5   1   1.5   2
Kilometres

ABOVE AND BELOW: Burrowye Camping Reserve

WALWA – TINTALDRA

This is a great area to fish for Murray cod and occasionally trout cod and brown trout. The Walwa Caravan Park is one of the best formal caravan parks on the Upper Murray and has modern cabins as well as full caravan and camping facilities. There is a concrete launching ramp here and the river is navigable (in all but very low levels) downstream for about one kilometre and upstream for about two kilometres.

This makes it a very popular fishery and you will see a large range of boats on the water here and many anglers will actually moor their boats in the river on the bank in the caravan park. Remember though, if you run the rapids downstream you will most likely have to continue downstream to Jingellic to retrieve. At water levels of 2 metres you should be able to navigate upstream and downstream with safety.

The areas at Neil's reserve, Clarke Lagoon and Tintaldra have easy areas to launch small tinnies, kayaks and canoes and will access anglers to some great fishing for Murray cod and brown trout. Land based access here is good both from the Victorian side along the Murray River Highway and the NSW side from River Road.

One great drift trip is to launch at Tintaldra and pull out at Clarke Lagoon (short day drift) or pull out at Neil's Reserve (long day drift). To do the drift (and actively fish) from Tintaldra to Walwa is too long a trip to get done in a day.

You cannot navigate far above the Tintaldra Bridge before encountering rapids. The area above Tintaldra to the junction of the Tooma River and beyond is a fabulous area for Murray cod.

BELOW: Walwa riverside caravan park

Walwa riverside

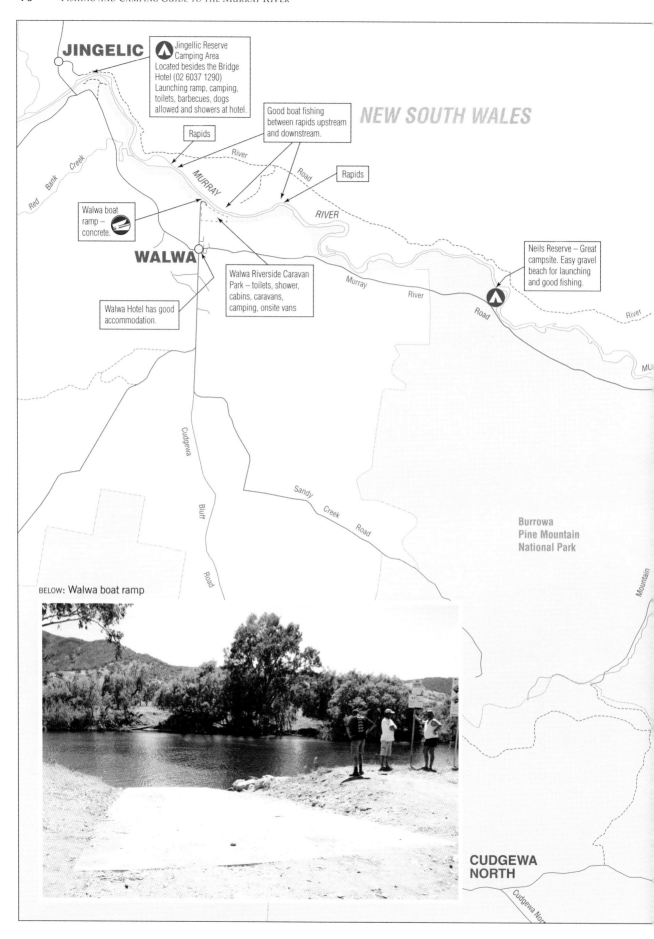

JINGELIC

Jingellic Reserve Camping Area
Located besides the Bridge Hotel (02 6037 1290) Launching ramp, camping, toilets, barbecues, dogs allowed and showers at hotel.

NEW SOUTH WALES

Good boat fishing between rapids upstream and downstream.

Rapids

Rapids

Red Bank Creek

River

MURRAY

Road

RIVER

Walwa boat ramp – concrete.

WALWA

Neils Reserve – Great campsite. Easy gravel beach for launching and good fishing.

Walwa Riverside Caravan Park – toilets, shower, cabins, caravans, camping, onsite vans

Murray

River

Road

River

Walwa Hotel has good accommodation.

MU

Cudgewa

Burrowa
Pine Mountain
National Park

Bluff

Sandy

Creek

Road

Road

Mountain

BELOW: Walwa boat ramp

CUDGEWA
NORTH

Cudgewa Nor

MAP 28 JINGELIC TO TINTALDRA

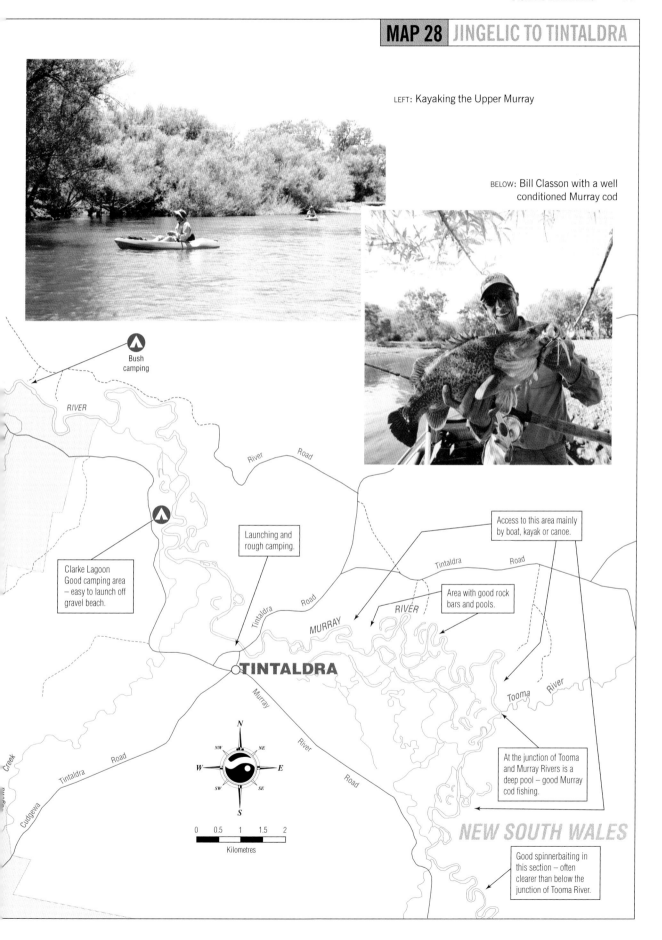

LEFT: Kayaking the Upper Murray

BELOW: Bill Classon with a well conditioned Murray cod

Bush camping

RIVER

River Road

Access to this area mainly by boat, kayak or canoe.

Launching and rough camping.

Tintaldra Road

Clarke Lagoon Good camping area – easy to launch off gravel beach.

Area with good rock bars and pools.

Tintaldra Road

MURRAY

RIVER

TINTALDRA

Murray River Road

Tooma River

At the junction of Tooma and Murray Rivers is a deep pool – good Murray cod fishing.

N
NW   NE
W   E
SW   SE
S

Creek

Tintaldra Road

Cudgewa

0   0.5   1   1.5   2
Kilometres

NEW SOUTH WALES

Good spinnerbaiting in this section – often clearer than below the junction of Tooma River.

Neils Reserve is a very popular area to camp right on the river bank.

The banks at Neils Reserve make for easy boat launching for small tinnies.

The area is well treed

Clarke Lagoon
Wildlife Reserve

⬦ WARNING

Limbs May Fall

Strong Currents

Submerged Objects

PARK INFORMATION 13 1963   Parks

ABOVE: Easy access at Clarke Lagoon is popular with caravanners.

BELOW: Clarke Lagoon also has easy launching.

TINTALDRA TO TOWONG UPPER

The river at Towong sees the transition from a Murray cod fishery to a predominantly trout fishery. Now, that doesn't mean there aren't cod above Towong and certainly vice versa, but it does give a general idea of how the river subtly changes.

Having said that the river downstream of its junction with the Corryong Creek has some of the best pools, rock bars and runs for Murray cod in the river! The pool downstream on the Murray from the Corryong offers great land based access for those chasing a Murray cod. From there downstream to Tintaldra however the access is very limited and you are best to fish this area from a canoe, kayak or tinnie and pull out at Tintaldra.

The section between Brigenbrong Bridge and Towong has at times some great trout fishing. It flows for the most part through private property, so it is best fishing from a drifting boat, raft or kayak. At water levels between .9 to 1.5 metres (there is a level indicator at Brigenbrong Bridge) the river is navigable downstream only. At 2 metres you can navigate both upstream and downstream in a small tinnie with an outboard motor. At this higher level one can motor upstream to the confluence with the Swampy Plains River.

It is a full day's drift from Brigenbrong and Towong

RIGHT: Tintaldra Hotel

BELOW: The junction of Corryong Creek and Upper Murray River

MAP 29 TINTALDRA TO TOWONG UPPER

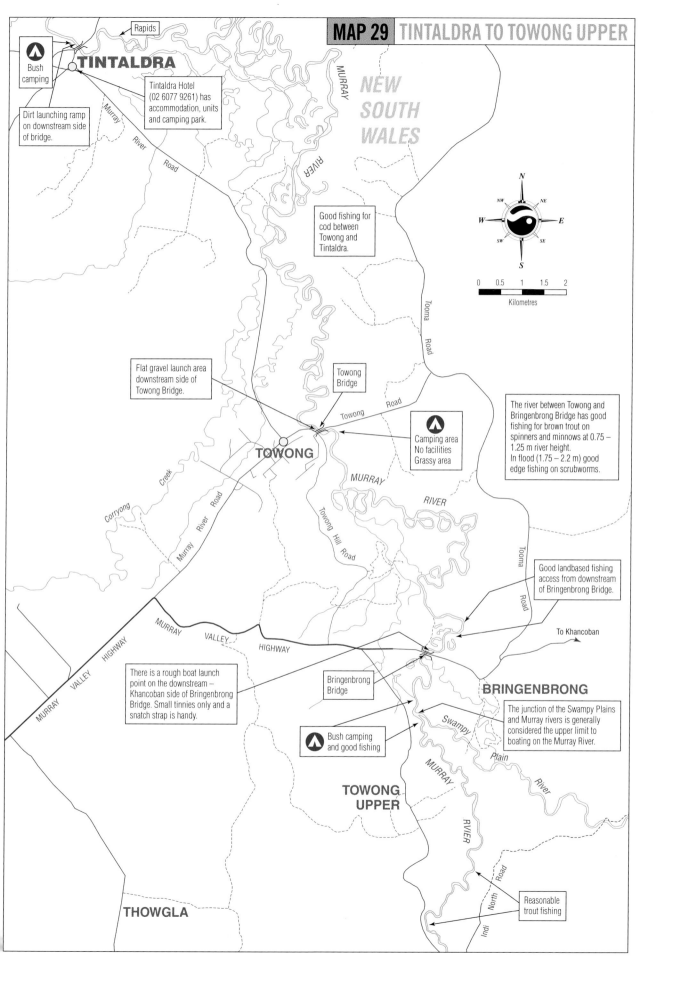

Rapids

Bush camping

TINTALDRA

Tintaldra Hotel (02 6077 9261) has accommodation, units and camping park.

Dirt launching ramp on downstream side of bridge.

Murray River Road

NEW SOUTH WALES

MURRAY RIVER

Good fishing for cod between Towong and Tintaldra.

Tooma Road

Flat gravel launch area downstream side of Towong Bridge.

Towong Bridge

Towong Road

Camping area No facilities Grassy area

The river between Towong and Bringenbrong Bridge has good fishing for brown trout on spinners and minnows at 0.75 – 1.25 m river height.
In flood (1.75 – 2.2 m) good edge fishing on scrubworms.

Corryong Creek

TOWONG

Murray River Road

MURRAY RIVER

Towong Hill Road

Tooma Road

Good landbased fishing access from downstream of Bringenbrong Bridge.

To Khancoban

MURRAY VALLEY HIGHWAY

MURRAY VALLEY HIGHWAY

There is a rough boat launch point on the downstream – Khancoban side of Bringenbrong Bridge. Small tinnies only and a snatch strap is handy.

Bringenbrong Bridge

BRINGENBRONG

The junction of the Swampy Plains and Murray rivers is generally considered the upper limit to boating on the Murray River.

Bush camping and good fishing

Swampy Plain River

TOWONG UPPER

MURRAY RIVER

Indi North Road

Reasonable trout fishing

THOWGLA

0 0.5 1 1.5 2
Kilometres

N
NW NE
W E
SW SE
S

ABOVE: Bush camping

LEFT: Upper Murray brown trout

RIGHT TOP: Drift fishing the Upper Murray

RIGHT BOTTOM: Camping on the Murray

and while casting from the boat is effective, at lower levels it is better to pull the boat up on the bank and fish the pools from the bank.

There are very few designated camp sites in this section – There is a lovely grassed area on the Murray at Towong that many campers and caravanners use and there are bush camps between the Brigenbrong Bridge and Upper Towong, although I suspect that land owners permission may need to be sought.

MAP 30 TOWING UPPER TO HAIRPIN BEND

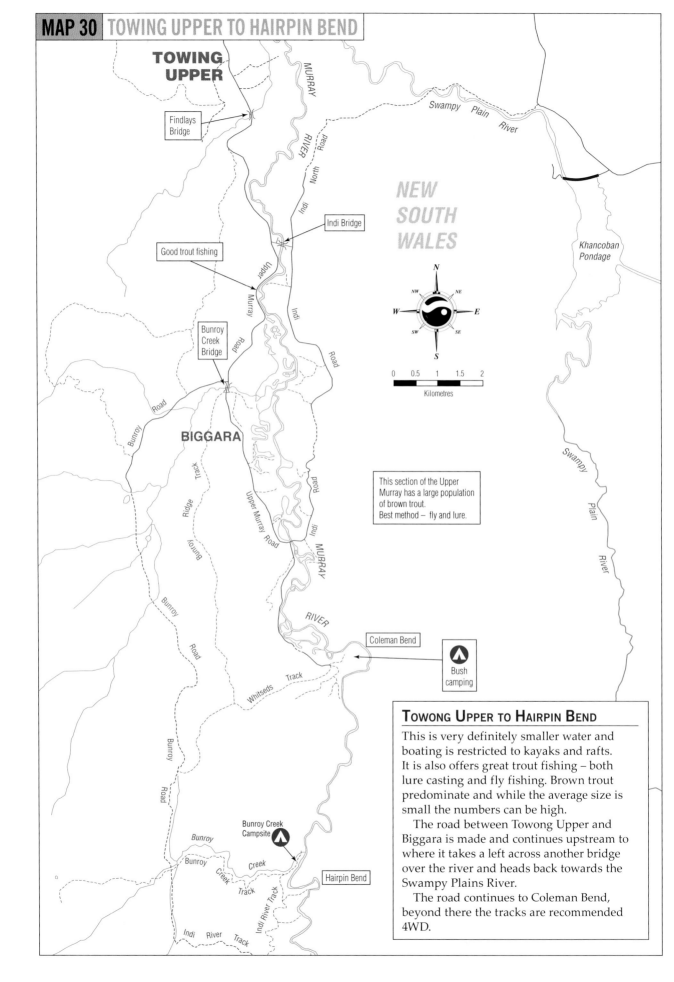

TOWING UPPER

Findlays Bridge

Indi Bridge

Good trout fishing

Bunroy Creek Bridge

BIGGARA

MURRAY RIVER

Indi North Road

Upper Murray Road

Indi Road

Bunroy Road

Bunroy Ridge Track

Bunroy Road

Whitseds Track

Bunroy Road

Bunroy Creek Campsite

Bunroy Creek Track

Indi River Track

Indi River Track

Hairpin Bend

Coleman Bend

Bush camping

NEW SOUTH WALES

Swampy Plain River

Khancoban Pondage

Swampy Plain River

N
NW NE
W E
SW SE
S

0   0.5   1   1.5   2
Kilometres

This section of the Upper Murray has a large population of brown trout.
Best method – fly and lure.

TOWONG UPPER TO HAIRPIN BEND

This is very definitely smaller water and boating is restricted to kayaks and rafts. It is also offers great trout fishing – both lure casting and fly fishing. Brown trout predominate and while the average size is small the numbers can be high.

The road between Towong Upper and Biggara is made and continues upstream to where it takes a left across another bridge over the river and heads back towards the Swampy Plains River.

The road continues to Coleman Bend, beyond there the tracks are recommended 4WD.

Hairpin Bend to Tom Groggin

The Fisherman's Bend Campsite is accessed via the Indi River Track from Biggara and is well known for its trout fishery. Trout are on average 300 to 500 grams. Bush camping at Fisherman's Bend, four wheel drive access only and no caravans.

The Hermit Creek camp site is well beyond and in a remote area of the Murray downstream of Tom Groggin Station and is definitely reached only with a 4WD.

There is no practical access to Tom Grogging Station and Tom Groggin Campsite from The Victorian side of the river. These areas are easily reached via the sealed Alpine Way from Khancoban.

Tom Groggin Station is located in a picturesque hidden valley through which the Murray River runs. The Station is private property and camping is not allowed without prior permission. Camping is allowed some 6 kilometres further south at Tom Groggin Campsite, right on the Murray and just off the Alpine Way.

RIGHT: The turn off to Tom Groggin Station from the Alpine Way.

BELOW: Tom Groggin Station is situated in one of the most beautiful upper Murray River valleys.

MAP 31 HAIRPIN BEND TO TOM GROGGIN

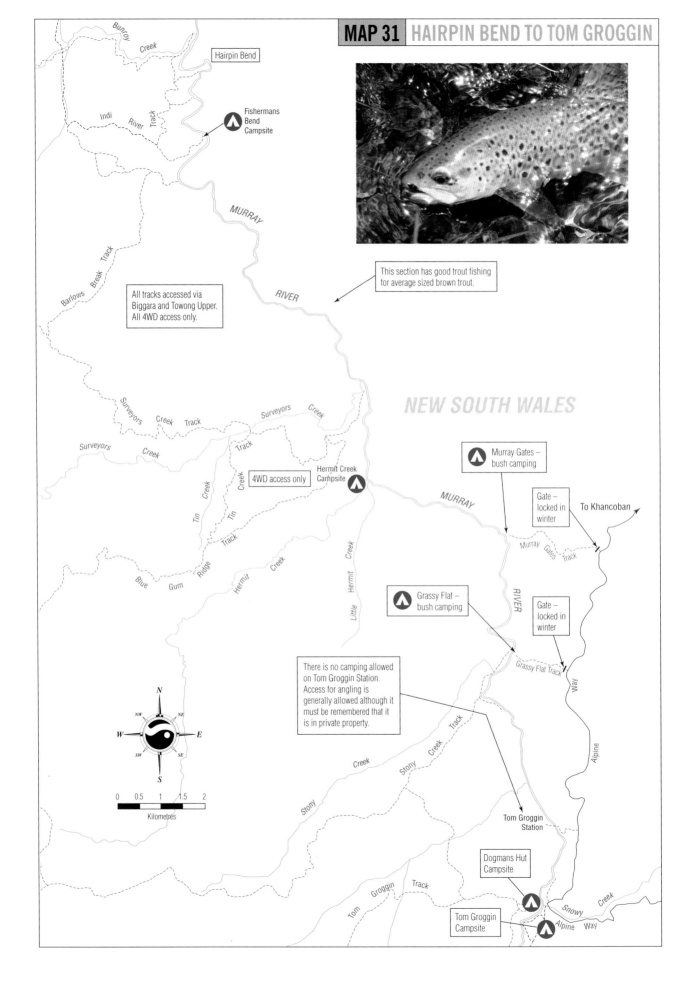

Hairpin Bend

Bunroy Creek

Indi River Track

Fishermans Bend Campsite

MURRAY

Barlows Break Track

RIVER

This section has good trout fishing for average sized brown trout.

All tracks accessed via Biggara and Towong Upper. All 4WD access only.

Surveyors Creek Track

Surveyors Creek

Surveyors Creek

NEW SOUTH WALES

Tin Creek

Tin Creek Track

Tin

4WD access only

Hermit Creek Campsite

Murray Gates – bush camping

MURRAY

Gate – locked in winter

To Khancoban

Murray Gates Track

Blue Gum Ridge

Hermit Creek

Little Hermit Creek

RIVER

Grassy Flat – bush camping

Gate – locked in winter

Grassy Flat Track

Way

There is no camping allowed on Tom Groggin Station. Access for angling is generally allowed although it must be remembered that it is in private property.

N
NW NE
W E
SW SE
S

0 0.5 1 1.5 2
Kilometres

Stony Creek Track

Stony Creek

Stony

Alpine

Tom Groggin Station

Dogmans Hut Campsite

Tom Groggin Track

Tom

Snowy Creek

Alpine Way

Tom Groggin Campsite

ABOVE: Upper Murray River has many rapids.

TOM GROGGIN TO ROUGH CREEK

The Tom Groggin Campsite is well known to travellers on the Alpine Way and is a lovely campsite that is popular in the summer months. The fishing there is reasonable – the further one ventures upstream the better.

There is a 4WD track over the river ford and onwards to the Davies Plain Track which then accesses the very upper part of the Murray River system. However most four wheel drivers will access this area from Benambra in Victoria.

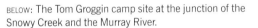

BELOW: The Tom Groggin camp site at the junction of the Snowy Creek and the Murray River.

BELOW: Entrance to the Tom Groggin campsite from the Alpine Way.

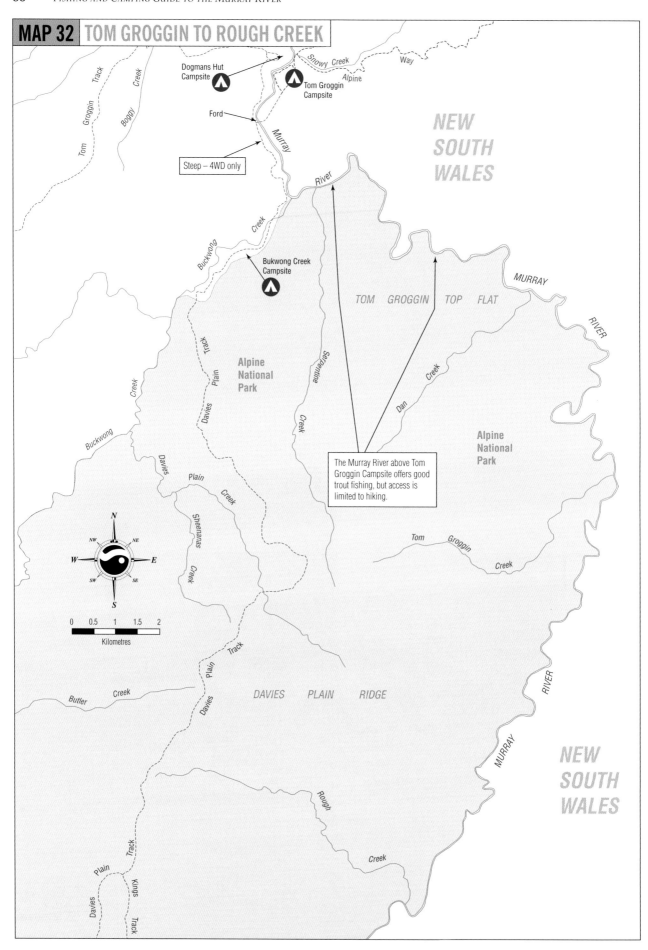

MAP 32 TOM GROGGIN TO ROUGH CREEK

Dogmans Hut
Campsite

Tom Groggin
Campsite

Ford

Snowy Creek

Alpine Way

Murray

Steep – 4WD only

River

NEW
SOUTH
WALES

Buckwong Creek
Campsite

TOM GROGGIN TOP FLAT

MURRAY

RIVER

Buckwong Creek

Alpine
National
Park

Track

Plain

Serpentine

Creek

Davies

Davies

Buckwong

Creek

Dan

Creek

Alpine
National
Park

The Murray River above Tom
Groggin Campsite offers good
trout fishing, but access is
limited to hiking.

Plain

Creek

Sheenanas

Creek

N
NW   NE
W   E
SW   SE
S

Tom   Groggin

Creek

0   0.5   1   1.5   2
Kilometres

Track

Plain

Davies

DAVIES PLAIN RIDGE

Butler   Creek

MURRAY

RIVER

NEW
SOUTH
WALES

Rough

Track

Plain

Davies

Kings

Track

Creek

UPPER MURRAY HEADWATERS

This does have some of the best trout fishing in the system with reports of occasional fish to over a kilo. However the average size would still only be 400 g. There is a nice bush camping area at the end of Kings Plain Track, remember that it is illegal to camp on the NSW side of the river.

The Poplars campsite is accessed via Davies Plain Track and then along McCarthy's Track. Here there is some good trout fishing both upstream and downstream and a serviceable bush campsite. The junction of Limestone Creek and the Murray River is the last campsite on the Upper Murray and is accessed via the Limestone Creek Track from Benambra. Bush camping is on the Limestone Creek before it's confluence with the Murray and often the flow in the Limestone is greater than that of the Murray River.

The Cowombat Flat campsite access has been blocked with a locked gate at Copperhead Creek.

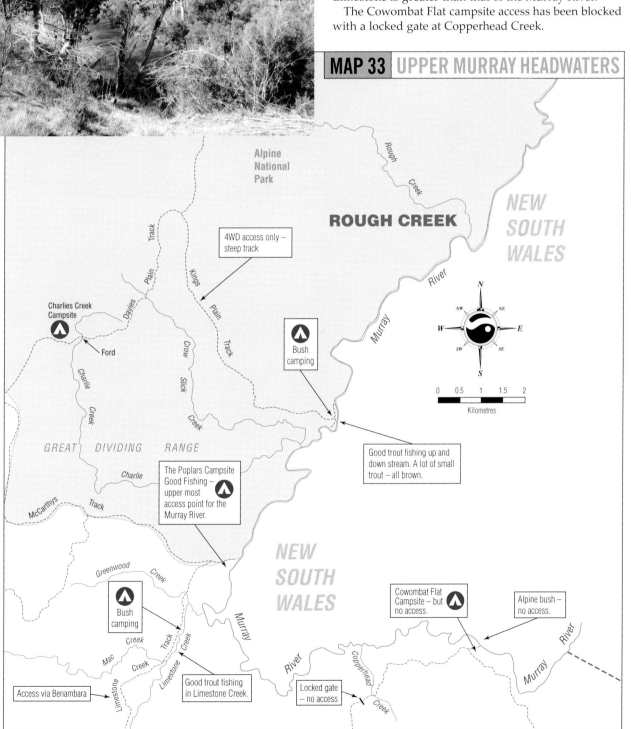

MAP 33 UPPER MURRAY HEADWATERS

Alpine National Park

Rough Creek

ROUGH CREEK

NEW SOUTH WALES

Track

Davies Plain

Kings Plain Track

Crow

Slick

Creek

4WD access only – steep track

Charlies Creek Campsite

Ford

Charlie Creek

Bush camping

Murray River

Good trout fishing up and down stream. A lot of small trout – all brown.

GREAT DIVIDING RANGE

Charlie

McCarthys Track

The Poplars Campsite Good Fishing – upper most access point for the Murray River.

Greenwood Creek

NEW SOUTH WALES

Bush camping

Mac Creek

Creek

Limestone

Track

Limestone Creek

Murray

River

Access via Benambra

Good trout fishing in Limestone Creek.

Cowombat Flat Campsite – but no access.

Alpine bush – no access.

Copperhead Creek

Murray River

Locked gate – no access

PART 3
FISHING THE MURRAY

THE LIFE AND TIMES OF MURRAY COD

The Murray cod is one of Australia's largest freshwater fish and is the second largest in the world. It has been known to grow to immense proportions, occasionally reaching 1.8 metres in length and well over 100 kilograms in weight, although fish of this size are unheard of in modern times.

The Murray cod has a number of different names. The most commonly used title is, of course, "Murray cod" or just plain "cod". It has, at other times, been referred to as "Goodoo", "Ponde" (pronounced Pon dee) and more colourfully as the "pig cod". This last name was given to cod caught in the Gunbower Creek region.

Murray cod were once a common fish. They were widely distributed throughout the freshwater rivers and streams of Eastern and Southern Australia. It was once believed that the cod were so common they would never run out. In fact, they were used as pig feed by earlier generations of Australians.

Today you are more likely to catch a fish of between two and five kilograms. The occasional fish weighing in excess of 45 kilograms can still be captured, but cod of this size are few and far between. Overfishing by commercial interests in the 1800s and early 1900s made massive inroads into the cod population. They are still harvested commercially today but on a much smaller scale and no new commercial licences are to be issued.

Further pressure has been placed on the cod by changes in environmental conditions. These changes were caused by the construction of dams and by changes to the flow of water in the rivers. Other changes, mostly caused by man, to the cod's habitat include such things as pollution, desnagging and siltation. All these factors have led to a huge decline in cod numbers. It is a decline that the cod has, so far, been unable to recover from without assistance from the source of the problem: man. Some forward thinking individuals, angling clubs and Government Departments have undertaken restocking programmes in an effort to halt and reverse the decline of the Murray cod.

The cod's breeding cycle starts in spring when the water temperature rises. The best breeding time is when the water is warm and the river is in flood. This allows the cod to spawn in the shallow, warmer water of the flooded swamps and grasslands surrounding the river. Cod reach maturity at the age of 4 to 5 years. The female can lay upwards of 40,000 eggs which hatch between one and two weeks later. The eggs are laid inside logs or in shallow water and are about 3mm in diameter. In their first few days of life the young cod are sustained by a yolk sack attached to their underside. They begin to feed themselves about a month after hatching. Murray cod grow quite quickly in their first few years of life. On average they can reach a weight of about five kilos and measure up to 64 centimetres in length in their fifth year.

DESCRIPTION

The Murray cod has a large head which is slightly flattened. It has small eyes and a short rounded snout. The jaws are usually equal in length but occasionally the lower jaw may protrude slightly. It has a large

mouth which extends laterally to below the eyes. They have very small teeth that feel more like very coarse sandpaper. Don't be fooled by this, they can inflict a nasty wound and have been known to draw blood. The cod's body is elongated and deep; the belly of the fish is pale, almost white, while the upper side and flanks are olive green to yellow green and have green mottled markings.

HABITAT

Murray cod inhabit the slow moving, turbid waters of the Murray Darling System and may be found in some impoundments if the water conditions are suitable.

They are likely to be found around areas that provide substantial cover, like fallen trees, overhanging banks and vegetation and other debris that has fallen into the river. Tree stumps and large rocks are also favoured by the cod. Combined with a steady flow of water and food these "snags" provide an ideal home for Murray cod of all sizes.

The importance of these snags cannot be overstated. The desnagging of our major rivers has been described as an environmental catastrophe and it is believed to have led to a proportional reduction of the fish population in the affected rivers. To put this in to perspective, between 1976 and 1987 in excess of 24,500 snags were removed from some sections of the Murray River. The removal of snags has become such a problem that a re-snagging programme has begun in some Victorian waterways.

Confluence of the Murrumbidgee River with the Murray River.

CATCHING A MURRAY COD

RODS, REELS AND LINE

Murray cod are hard fighting fish and can grow to very large sizes so light gear might not be up to the job of landing your catch. Also the rod and reel used when bait fishing for cod may not be suitable for trolling lures. Some anglers prefer to use a short, stout, boat rod when bait fishing, others may prefer to use a slightly longer, more flexible rod. When trolling lures it is wise to use a rod that will telegraph the action of the lure. I prefer to use a Mako rod coupled with a Shimano Calcutta and a braided line. Mako rods are custom made by Bob Darley of Shepparton in Victoria. Bob builds a good range of reasonably priced rods.

Match your rod with an appropriately sized threadline or baitcaster reel; some folks may even prefer to use a side cast model. Generally speaking though the reel should have the capacity to take fairly heavy line. When bait fishing, a heavier line is advisable as you will be fishing in and around the snags and cod are very quick to find cover when hooked. Line with a breaking strain of about 10kg is fine. With lures however you can use a slightly lighter line, up to about 8 kilograms. There will be some sport fishermen reading this who are probably cringing at the thought of using heavy line. But there are likely to be many more weekend anglers who will feel a good deal safer using heavier gear. Research has shown that a fish is more likely to survive when released if it can be returned to the water quickly with a minimum of stress. Obviously this is more likely to be achieved by using a heavier line, but that decision is up to you.

BAIT FISHING

The first thing you need to do when chasing a cod is to locate a likely looking snag. Ideally your snag would cause the water to swirl and eddy around it. Sometimes not all of the snag will be visible above the water and it will only be indicated by a small branch or twig. The size of the underwater structure is sometimes shown by the water flow. The sign of a reasonably large snag is turbulent water downstream of the small branch or twig. Extreme caution is required when boating in these areas as very large fallen trees may be lying just beneath the surface of the water and out of view of the boaters. These are known, rather colourfully, as "widow makers". Sunglasses with polarised lenses are a great help when negotiating these areas. Once you've picked out your snag you need to anchor up or tie off about 10 to 20 metres upstream.

There are a wide variety of baits for cod; there is an equally wide variety of ways to rig these baits. I don't know all of them but I do know which ones have worked for me in the past and are still working for me now.

RIGS

Using the KISS formula (Keep It Simple Stupid) when bait fishing for Murray cod makes good sense. There are two very simple rigs that we use: first, the Running Sinker rig and secondly, the Paternoster rig.

The Running Sinker rig has two variations. In the first the sinker is allowed to run down to the eye of the

LEFT: Ben Snowden with a medium sized Murray cod.

ABOVE: The author, Brian Hinson with a Murray cod.

hook. This is a very effective rig when used in the snags as the sinker can assist in unsnagging the hook. When the hook becomes snagged simply lift the rod tip sharply. This causes the sinker to shoot up the line a short distance, then fall back on to the eye of the hook, disengaging it from the snag. The second running sinker rig involves the use of a swivel and a 40 to 50cm nylon trace.

The Paternoster Rig also has two

Running sinker rig

Red beads

40–50 cm of 4 or 5 kg nylon trace

Swivel

Running sinker

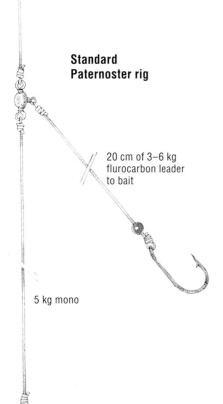

Standard Paternoster rig

20 cm of 3–6 kg flurocarbon leader to bait

5 kg mono

Fixed teardrop sinker

Yabby rig with 2 sinkers

variations, you have the one hook or two hook variety. It is simply a matter of attaching the sinker to the end of the line and have one or two 20cm droppers above the sinker. The one hook variety is usually better when fishing in snaggy areas because there is no second hook to become snagged while you are fighting your trophy cod.

The Paternoster Rig is very effective during the winter when the crayfish are on the move. It helps to lift the bait off the bottom and keeps it out of reach of all but the biggest of crayfish.

The hook pattern and size that you use will depend on the type and size of your bait. As far as size is concerned, a hook in the size range 1 to 4/0 will be suitable. The hook pattern that I use is of the "wide gape" variety such as the Mustad All Rounder.

Sinkers are another item of terminal tackle that can vary depending on the fishing conditions. A lighter sinker is preferable but don't be scared of using a heavy sinker in very fast water. In 99% of cases the running sinker is the preferred method because it allows the fish to take the bait without feeling any resistance.

Two sinkers rigged between 2 brass rings will send out sonic signals when the rig is bounced.

THE BAIT

There are various baits that can be used to catch Murray cod. The most commonly used baits are bardi grubs, yabbies, worms and shrimps, in that order. Less commonly used baits are a piece of red meat or freshwater mussels. Some folks believe that the shrimp are attracted to the red meat and this, in turn, becomes a delicious meal for the Murray cod. They are also very partial to small live carp, *but* in some states it is illegal to use live finned fish as bait, so remember to check at your local tackle outlet or with your local fisheries officer. It goes without saying that the fresher the bait the better it is.

BARDI GRUBS

Make sure the hook size is appropriate for the size of grub being used. Start by threading the point of the hook into the grub at a point underneath the head and between the legs. Thread the hook all the way through the grub until the barb is exposed. You can secure the grub to the hook by using a half hitch around the head or by wrapping a length of cotton or very fine fuse wire around the body of the grub and the hook. Another method of securing the grub to the hook is by the use a couple of very small rubber bands. Place the rubber bands over the grubs head and tail and then thread the hook under them. This method allows you to reclaim your grub at the end of the session.

Recently a young man from Rochester in Victoria came up with an ingenious method of preserving the grub when used as bait. Called "The Grub Saver", it is a hollow latex mould of a bardi grub. It slides over your bait and prevents the theft of your bait by smaller fish, yabbies and other bait robbers, while still allowing the natural smell of the grub to permeate the water. This

Cleared leaf mould showing holes and the extracted bardi grubs.

has the added benefit of saving you some money with the cost of bardi grubs being anywhere between $1 and $2 each!

YABBIES

As with bardi grubs, make sure that the hook you are using is of a suitable size.

The most common way of putting the yabbie on the hook is to thread the hook through the yabbie's tail. Start at a point just under the tail fan and slide the hook down through the tail to a point just before the legs below the carapace. The hook exits the tail here. Push the hook through far enough to expose the barb. Be very careful not damage the dark vein in the tail as this will cause the yabbie to die very quickly. Alternatively you can push the hook through the tail from to bottom to top just below the tail fan. When using the yabbie in this way ensure the sinker is allowed to slide right down to the eye of the hook. This method gives excellent results when used for bobbing in the snags. The yabbie will remain active when pinned like this. The hook can be easily removed without harming them.

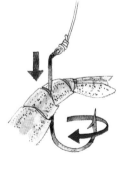

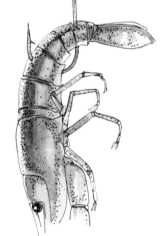

Bardi grubs are the best bait for Murray cod, fresh or frozen.

Another option involves the use of rubber bands again. Simply place the rubber bands over the yabbies tail and thread your hook under them. This keeps your yabbie alive for a lot longer. There is no need to remove the rubber bands from the yabbie at the end of the day as they will not harm it in any way. Because, in the last two methods described, the yabbies stay alive, they are able to crawl around naturally. While this may be a good thing as far as attracting the fish's attention is concerned, it allows them to crawl into holes and snags and thereby costing you your rig. You can prevent this by lightly crushing either the carapace or nose of the yabbie.

OTHER BAITS

There are a number of other baits that can be used to catch cod. These are worms, shrimp and freshwater mussels.

Shrimp are the best of the rest. They can be used dead or alive. However when used for cod it is best to use them in numbers. A largish hook with a cluster of shrimp makes an excellent alternative when your grubs or yabbies aren't doing the trick. Thread your first shrimp on in much the same way as you did the yabbie, from the tail fan to the legs. Then, thread on a couple more, pass the hook through the body from side to side and if possible have them facing each other.

When using worms, put as many worms on the hook as you can making sure that there are plenty of wriggly ends and the point and barb are not obstructed.

Freshwater mussels are a natural food item for cod but one that is rarely used as bait these days. The

Swivel

30–40 cm
of 3 kg
flurocarbon

Running sinker
above coloured
beads

Beads

Single large
scrub worm or
multiple garden
or tiger worms

**Rig for bobbing
worms for active
fishing**

reason for this is unclear but may have something to do with availability. The mussel beds become exposed when the water level in the river is very low. This is also true of irrigation channels where they can also be found. To use the mussel as bait you need to remove the fleshy part from the shell. Place your hook through the firmest part of the flesh and thread the remainder over the hook a number of times. The softest parts of the flesh will be picked off in quick time by the smaller fish.

You have now found your spot and rigged your bait, all that remains to be done is for you to get your bait to where the fish are.

BAIT FISHING TECHNIQUES

Cast your bait back towards the snag allowing the sinker to stop just short of it. This will allow your bait to wave around in the current close to the snag and in the cod's "strike zone". In very rough country set your bait about a metre short of the snag. This will entice the cod out of its lair and put you on more even terms as far as the ensuing fight is concerned. You should try to avoid casting into the snag as you will lose countless rigs and make it extremely difficult for you to extract any fish that you may hook

Fishing with your bait just out of the cod's reach calls for the use of some kind of enticement to be added to your bait. There are a number of scent additives around but I have found the best to be a liberal dousing with CRC.

It should be noted that the cod's bite is not always aggressive and occasionally it may be nothing more than a gentle bending of the rod as the cod lifts the bait and swims off with it. Once you've set your bait check that the line is fairly taut as this will allow you to quickly gain control of the fish once he has been hooked. Cod are very quick and strong. Once hooked, they can be back under cover in a flash and often catch the unwary off guard. If you can gain control of the fish early in the piece then the rest of the fight will be that much easier. It is a good idea to keep the rod tip high and use the rod to absorb the pressure of the fish, this also helps you keep it out of the snags and off the bottom.

I believe that 90% of fish are lost at the boat or bank as a lot of fisherman are not prepared for the fish's last desperate lunge. It is at this point where another pair of hands is a bonus as they can help you to land the fish. Once the fish is subdued lead it to the net and not the net to the fish. Lead it in head first as this will avert disaster should the fish regain some fire and start thrashing around once in the net.

LURES

The range of lures available on the market today is truly mind boggling! They come in a wondrous array of shapes, sizes and colours. I've heard it said that lures catch more fisherman than fish. This might be true and I often wonder how some of the more outlandishly coloured lures that I see in tackle stores will ever catch a fish, but they do!

DEVELOPMENTS

Early cod lures were large, heavy, mechanical, monsters called "Aeroplane spinners". They could be bought at your local tackle store but usually they were constructed from various bits and pieces found around the home, with the blades fashioned from jam tin lids or flattened penny coins. Often heavy and ungainly these lures required heavy line to tow them and they were prone to snagging. Some forward thinking anglers

Good sized Murray cod caught on a Hammerhead lure.

of the day attached a short length of bicycle wheel spoke to the front of the lure. This pointed forward and assisted the spinner in negotiating the snags. The idea was that the bicycle spoke would strike the snag first and flip the spinner up and over the snag. Aeroplane spinners are still used by some anglers today however they are notorious for twisting nylon line.

Lure fishing for Murray cod was revolutionised by the introduction of the rubber bodied "Flopys". They were ahead of their time with their adjustable bibs which could be raised or lowered to suit any fishing situation. Development of lures over the last 15 to 20 years has followed a common theme, but there is a wide variety of colours, shapes, sizes and actions available on the market today

There is a vast range of lures used to catch Murray cod. The majority of them are bibbed, which causes the lure to dive. The style and shape of the bib determines two things: firstly, how deep the lure will dive and secondly the action of the lure.

As already stated there are many brand names to choose from and all have their idiosyncrasies. But one brand of lures that is truly versatile is JJ's Stumpjumpers, manufactured by John Ellis of Cobram, Victoria. Any of the Stumpjumper lures can be altered to suit any fishing situation. This is due to the ingenious interchangeable bib system.

A keen Murray cod fisherman will have many lures in his armoury and he will usually have a favourite colour, shape or brand. The type of lure you use to catch a cod will depend on the particular fishing situation in which you find yourself. There are no hard and fast rules attached to lure fishing for cod and a lure that works one day may not work the next. As strange as it may sound darker lures seem to work better on very dull days or at night.

SPINNERBAITS

Spinnerbaits have become very popular since the first edition of *Fishing the Murray River* hit the bookstands. There are now many brands on the market. I am by no means an expert, but I have caught many native fish of all sizes on these exciting lures.

The range of colours and shapes available in spinnerbaits can be a little overwhelming—wish bone, quad spin, twin spin, Colorado blades, willow leaf blades, tandem blades and the different colours of the blades and skirts.

The most productive colour skirts that I have found are purple/white, orange/green and red/black. All of these have been very effective in the Murray River.

The blade colour is largely an individual's preference. I prefer silver on bright, sunny days as it reflects more, and gold in the milky Murray water has worked best for me. I prefer Colorado blades for their slower sinking rate and the greater vibration that they emit on a slow retrieve helps in the discoloured water.

They come in various weights, and the weight used depends a lot on the current where you are fishing. I mainly use weights of 3/8 to 5/8 oz while casting in slow to fast water, but I use weights up to 2.5 oz when trolling.

All of my spinnerbaits have a stinger (or trailing) hook attached with a soft plastic threaded on.

When using a spinnerbait I look for a big tree sloping down into the river, big snags lying parallel to the bank or a ledge with a sharp drop-off. But there are many other places that our native fish can be found waiting.

On casting a spinnerbait into the strike zone I usually count as it sinks until it hits the bottom. This gives me an idea when to start the retrieve on subsequent casts so that it is just above the bottom. Upon starting a slow retrieve I usually twitch the rod tip slightly (about 10 cm) and allow it to fall again. I continue this erratic action all the way back to the boat. The hookups

Good size Murray cod caught on an Outlaw Spinnerbait.

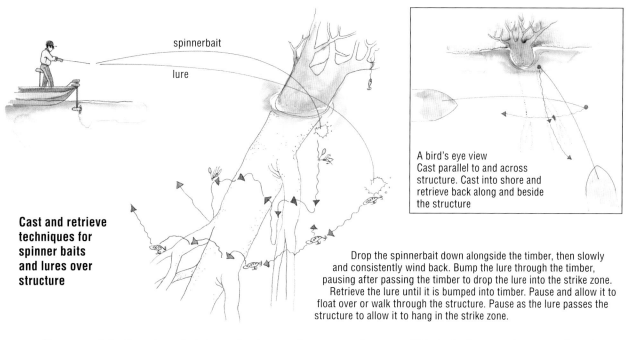

spinnerbait

lure

A bird's eye view
Cast parallel to and across
structure. Cast into shore and
retrieve back along and beside
the structure

**Cast and retrieve
techniques for
spinner baits
and lures over
structure**

Drop the spinnerbait down alongside the timber, then slowly
and consistently wind back. Bump the lure through the timber,
pausing after passing the timber to drop the lure into the strike zone.
Retrieve the lure until it is bumped into timber. Pause and allow it to
float over or walk through the structure. Pause as the lure passes the
structure to allow it to hang in the strike zone.

usually come while the spinnerbait is on the drop, so be prepared.

Another effective retrieve is to cast out, let the spinnerbait drop and start a slow retrieve, allowing the spinnerbait to drop after every 4 or 5 turns of the handle, then continue the slow retrieve.

When using spinnerbaits be prepared for a strike at any time—especially on the drop.

We have all been amazed at the number of spinnerbait manufacturers on the market as well as the 'backyarders' trying to get in on it. I stick to the well known brands these days and Outlaw Spinnerbaits would be one of the best. Outlaw have a variety of coloured skirts, various blades and head weights, with a special one called a six shooter. So if you want to give spinnerbaits a try, I suggest you stick to the better brands, as I have had many lesser known brands break and lost prized natives.

Give spinnerbaits a go — it is a great way to catch our prized native fish.

LURE FISHING TECHNIQUES

There are a couple of different ways in which you can use lures when fishing for cod. The first of these is the cast and retrieve method and the second is by trolling your lures behind the boat. When casting lures it is vital that your lure reaches the "strike zone" quickly. A lot of lures take sometime and distance to reach the required depth. As this is the case you will find that by the time your lure is at the right depth it is well and truly outside the area where the cod may be. You might find that casting your lure just beyond the snag before you start the retrieve may assist you in getting it into the right spot. Alternatively use a lure that dives quickly. A lure that is both a quick diver and floats when at rest is ideal. Floating lures are much easier to unsnag. When you feel the lure hitting the snags, halt your retrieve and allow the line to become slack. Nine times out of ten this will allow your lure to float up and

over the snags. This isn't always going to work and you will need some kind of desnagging device to help you out. We will talk about these a little bit later on.

The other method of using lures is by trolling them behind a boat in close to the snags and structures. This method requires a degree of skill, and a knowledge of the water in which you are fishing. You will be greatly aided by a fish finder or depth sounder that gives you a clear picture of the bottom and help you locate the snags and other structures where fish lurk.

A soft tipped rod is my choice when trolling lures as this allows the movement of the lure to be transmitted up the line, through the rod to your finger tips. This has the added benefit of transmitting the vibration of your line rubbing on snags before the lure becomes snagged.

When trolling lures hold your fishing rod so that it is pointing slightly forward. If all is well the action of your lure is signalled by the quivering of the rod tip. If the rod tip is not quivering your lure is probably not "swimming" correctly. This may be caused by any of a number of factors, such as the line and hooks becoming tangled, the line, hook or lure being fouled by weed or debris or the lure hitting the bottom. Whatever the reason it will pay you to check the lure and take corrective action as required. If the lure becomes snagged when trolling, allow the rod tip to move rearward, this may be enough to release the lure from the snag. It may also be necessary for you to stop the boat otherwise its forward momentum may prevent your lure from floating free of the snag. If your lure becomes well and truly stuck on a snag it's time to break out the trusty desnagging device. Again, as with most fishing tackle, there are a number of proprietary models available and they are all very good, but I have found them wanting in the faster flowing water. I use a fairly large shackle, about 15cm long, attached to some heavy cord. This is used in the same way as the other models but has the added benefit of extra weight to help free those stubborn lures.

Murray cod of 60–80 cm are being caught more frequently in the Murray River. Ron Robertson caught this nice conditioned cod on an Outlaw Spinnerbait

Direction of travel when trolling may seem unimportant when fishing still waters, however when fishing in rivers it can play quite a major role in the retrieval of snagged lures. Travelling against the current has a couple of advantages over trolling downstream such as assisting in slowing the boat's momentum and helping the lure float backwards out of the snag in the direction from which it came.

The current can also help in controlling the speed of the boat. The boat speed needs to be adjusted to make the lure swim in the right way and also to change the action of the lure slightly. This slight change may be all that is needed to tempt the fish. When heading downstream however, you will generally be at the mercy of the current and you may not be able to troll at the right speed; also you may not be able stop soon enough to prevent the lure from becoming snagged.

A question I am often asked is "how far behind the boat should I drag my lure"? Generally speaking, there is no set distance. This all depends on the depth of the water and the diving action of the lure. It is in this area that the Stumpjumper lures come into their own as they have interchangeable bibs, so an old favourite or even a successful lure can be used at a variety of depths. A good planning distance though would be ten to fifteen metres behind the boat. If you feel the lure strike the bottom, quickly lift the rod tip to help the lure over the bump. If, however, the lure is continually hitting the bottom this would indicate that you are dragging the lure too far back or your lure is diving too deep. This can be resolved by shortening the distance back to the lure or by changing the lure or bib.

A factor you should take into account when fishing with lures is that each is finely tuned to "swim" in a certain way. This action can be affected by such things as swivels, heavy nylon line and the type of knot used. When attaching your lure it is advisable to use a loop knot as this causes little or no hindrance to the lure's action. When using a braided line, as I do, it can become a costly exercise to use eight to ten inches of line when making the loops. Multiply this by the number of times you change your lure in a session and you can see that your expensive line will become a good deal shorter by the end of a days fishing. This can be alleviated by joining a few feet of nylon line to the end of your braided line. Knot selection when joining the braided and nylon line is also very important.

There are many techniques used to catch cod. No doubt they are all successful. The techniques described here are the ones that I have found to be the most useful over 40 years of fishing, and while the rods, reels and lines have all undergone technological advances these techniques have only been adapted to take advantage of the those changes.

BASIC KNOTS

Arbor Knot

This is a very fast and secure knot for attaching line to the reel. Pass the tag end of the line around the spool and form an overhand knot with the tag end around the main line. Then another overhand knot on the tag end of the line. Lubricate the knots if using monofilament, tighten down by pulling the main line, and trim the tag.

Clinch Knot

Thread the line through the hook eye and wrap the end back up the line five times. Thread the leader back through the first loop in front of the hook eye. Lubricate the knot and pull steadily to tighten it against the hook eye. When tightening, hold the tag end of the tippet against the hook to avoid knot slippage. Trim the tag end.

Trilene Knot

A strong knot for tying medium hooks to 6–15 kg line. Thread the line through the hook eye twice and wrap it back up the line five times. Thread the line back through the two loops formed at the hook eye. Lubricate the knot and pull steadily to tighten the knot against the eye of the hook. When tightening, hold the tag end of the line against the hook to avoid knot slippage. Trim the tag and the end of the line.

Uni Knot

An easy-to-tie versatile knot. Thread the eye of the hook with the line so that the hook is suspended on a loop. Encircle the main line with the tag so another loop is formed. Wrap the double strand inside the loop with the tag protruding from the loop. Close the knot but do not pull it tight just yet. Slide the knot down onto the hook, pull it tight and trim the tag.

Homer Rhode Knot

This knot should never be used on lighter weight monofilaments, as it breaks at around 50 per cent of the line test.

Step One

Form an overhand knot in the main line leaving approximately 20 cm of monofilament between the knot and the tag end. Pass the tag end through the hook eye and then back through the overhand knot from the same side as it exited.

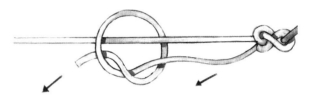

Step Two

Tighten the overhand knot lightly to the hook eye by pulling on the tail of the hook and on the tag end of the line, while keeping the two lines parallel to prevent the hook from twisting on the knot. Make another overhand knot over the standing part of the line. This knot is the stopper for the loop, so its position determines the size of the loop. Generally this knot would be 2–3 cm from the hook eye.

Step Three

Tighten this second knot and then pull on the bend of the hook and the main line at the same time. The knot at the hook eye should slide up the line snugly into the second knot. Trim the tag.

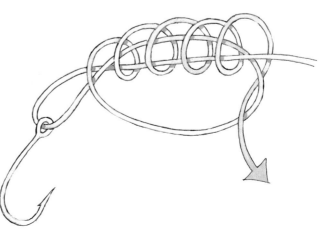

Double Surgeon's Knot

The quickest knot for joining two sections of leader and is especially useful when the sections are very different in diameter.

Overlap two sections of line about 15 cm. Form a 5 cm loop and tie in three overhand knots through the large loop. Lubricate the knot and pull steadily on all four ends to tighten. Trim the tag ends closely to the formed knot.

This knot is often used to form a dropper, but is best used only when speed is of the essence as the Blood Knot males a better dropper by allowing the droppers to stand at right angles to the main line.

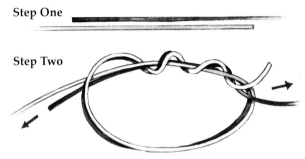

Blood Knot

This is the most frequently used knot for joining two sections of like-diameter monofilament.

Cross two 5 cm lengths of line over each other and hold the cross formed with your right thumb and forefinger. Use your left hand to make five turns with the short end of the line around the long section, twisting away from your thumb and forefinger. Bring back the short end and insert it through the other side of the crossed lines.

Now switch the knot over from your right to left thumb and forefinger, and repeat the process using the left tag end. Bring the tag back as before and tread it through the centre loop formed, but in the opposite direction to the right hand tag.

Lubricate the loose knot with saliva and draw the knot tight before trimming the tag ends close to the knot.

This knot makes an excellent dropper knot. When you start to tie this knot, simply allow one of the tag ends to be about 15–30 cm ling. At the completion of the knot, trim the short tag end only, leaving the longer tag for the dropper.

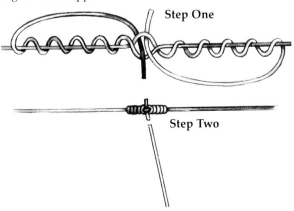

Albright Knot

The Albright Knot is a standard knot and is used when joining lines that are very different in diameter or when joining wire to monofilament.

Form a loop in the tag end of the heavier line or wire making sure you allow 15 cm to overlap. Take the lighter line and pass the tag through the formed loop. Pinch both lines about 8 cm from the end, and at the same time allow approximately 8 cm of the lighter line to protrude beyond this point to tie the knot. Start winding the lighter line back towards the end loop. Make at least ten tight turns of the lighter material back over the doubled section. Pass the lighter material through the end of the loop on the same side of the loop that the lighter line originally entered.

Very slowly, pull on the lighter line ends while grasping the heavier section and working the coils of the knot towards the loop end. Do not allow the coils to slip off the loop. Take special care when tying this knot as it is very prone to slipping if not tightened correctly.

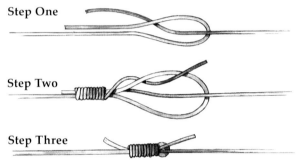

Double Line Knot

This knot can be tied using monofilament or braid and is a simple double line loop knot where you may require extra line strength.

Make a loop by overlapping the tag end of the line back onto the main line, bringing the tag end back by about 60 cm. Make nine to ten wraps around the main line away from the loop end.

Now take the same number of loops back towards the loop. On one arm of the main loop tie an overhand knot, lubricate the overhand knot and draw it tight.

Tie an overhand knot on the opposite arm of the main loop, lubricate the overhand knot and draw it tight.

Trim off the tag.

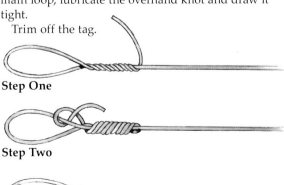

OTHER NATIVE FISH

Trout Cod

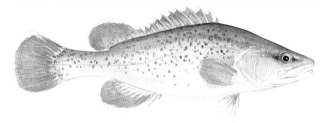

The trout cod is an endangered species and is totally protected

The trout cod, also called the "blue cod" or "blue nosed cod", is a similar species to the other freshwater cod such as Murray cod, Mary River cod and the eastern cod.

Description

The trout cod is similar in appearance to the Murray cod but there are some major differences. The trout cod has an overhanging upper jaw, the head has a straight profile with few markings and has a very pronounced stripe through the eye. The belly of the fish is white and the upper side and flanks have spotted markings which are blue/grey in colour. They do not grow as big as Murray cod.

Habitat

Trout cod live in similar surroundings to the Murray cod. The larger fish prefer to hang about in deep holes but the smaller fish prefer to hide in snags.

Their distribution is now very limited. They have been subjected to the same environmental pressures as the Murray cod but this has resulted in a more dramatic fall in numbers. At present, there is only one self-maintaining population of trout cod in the Murray River—between Yarrawonga and Tocumwal. Special

fishing regulations apply in this section of the river: fishing is not permitted from the first of September to midnight on the last day of November. When fishing is allowed you may only use one fishing rod with a maximum of two hooks attached. If trout cod are caught they must be immediately released. The taking or attempted taking of trout cod from Victorian waters is prohibited.

Golden Perch

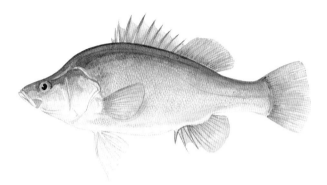

The golden perch is known variously as "yellowbelly" or "callop" and less commonly as the "white perch".

The golden perch was a very common fish that occurred throughout the Murray Darling system and many other waterways of inland Australia. They are less common these days, again, environmental changes caused by man have resulted in the decline of this fish. The regulation of water flow by dams and other structures has had an adverse effect on the fish. These structures have prevented the migration of many native fish, caused a lowering of the water temperature and changed the conditions of the rivers. This in turn has affected the breeding cycle of the golden perch. Government authorities have recognised this problem and have instigated a programme of restocking and have begun constructing "fish ladders" at some weirs. This will enable large scale natural breeding to occur once more.

Golden perch are known travellers. Before the river flows were regulated, golden perch would travel widely. Tagged golden perch were commonly recorded moving over 1000 km and once a "Yella" was known to have swum more than 2000 kilometres.

Description

The colour of golden perch can vary between olive green, bronze, yellow and white depending on its habitat and water colour. It has large eyes and a convex head. The mouth is quite large and extends to just behind the eye. The back is humped and this becomes very pronounced in larger fish. The gill covers have a sharp serrated edge and have a particularly vicious spike that can cause a nasty wound. Fish caught in impoundments are generally larger than river fish.

Trout cod take the same bait and live in the same area as Murray cod. This little trout cod was caught on a Stumpjumper size 2.

HABITAT

The golden perch is found in most inland rivers and impoundments. It prefers warm, turbid and sluggish water and is able to endure extremes of temperature and water conditions. They like the cover of snags and undercut banks. Golden perch prefer to lie in wait and ambush their prey as it passes, but they will also move around in open water and grassy shores looking for food. Always check out the snags first when fishing for "yellas".

Golden perch spawn in warmer water. Spawning is triggered by spring and summertime floods and when the water temperatures reaches or exceeds 20 degrees Celsius. The female, who may lay over 500,000 eggs, is able to retain her eggs until water conditions become suitable for spawning.

HOW TO CATCH A GOLDEN PERCH

BAIT

Golden perch will readily take a number of different baits and lures. The best baits for golden perch are small live yabbies, anything up to about 5cm in length will do. Next best would be live shrimp, followed by the humble earthworm and finally a cocktail of worms

and shrimps. Although fresh live bait is undoubtedly the way to go, dead baits may also be used. For example you can remove the carapace shell from dead yabbies leaving the tail and legs, these are known as "spiders" and can be deadly when bobbed in the "snags". When shrimp die they turn a milky white colour. Do not discard these as they are also excellent bait and can be used in your worm/shrimp cocktail or placed on a hook with a live shrimp. To top it all off and as strange as it may sound, a liberal coating of CRC will help attract the fish. If you don't believe me give it a try! Golden perch are generally timid biters when the bait is stationary but they will attack the bait aggressively when it is moved.

LURES

Golden perch will attack lures with gusto. They have been known to take lures almost as big as themselves. They will generally sideswipe the lure first and then attack it again from underneath. This is when most hook ups occur. I have noticed that most of the golden perch I have caught are hooked on the front trebles on larger lures.

Lures in the colour ranges of yellow, green, and red are my preferred choice and over the years I have had most success using lures with these base colours or a combination of these colours. Golden perch prefer a lure up to 100mm in length with a tight shimmying action.

RODS AND REELS

Over the years I have found that a light to medium rod of about 1.8m in length with a sensitive tip to be the most functional. A mid sized "eggbeater" or small baitcasting reel and line with breaking strain of up to 4.5 kg becomes an ideal set up for both lure casting and bait fishing in and around the snags.

RIGS

The style of rig that you use when fishing for golden perch depends on the type of water you are fishing. Generally speaking though, there are three rigs that are most commonly used around the Murray. The style of hook you use is really up to you, but I have found that the wide gape style of hook such as the Mustad All Rounder from size 4 to 2/0, to be a good choice.

As the rules and regulations governing fishing for Golden Perch vary from state to state, it is wise to check with your local tackle outlet or fisheries inspector before venturing out.

LEFT: Many anglers, like Ashley Barber, have found that targeting golden perch in the Murray can be very rewarding.

SILVER PERCH

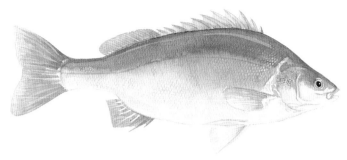

The silver perch is also known as the "black bream" or "silver bream". Like many other Australian native fish its numbers have fallen sharply as result of changed environmental conditions. Again, like other Australian native fish they are the focus of restocking programmes and are found throughout the Murray-Darling system. In New South Wales, silver perch can only be taken on a catch and release basis.

DESCRIPTION

The silver perch has a small head and small eyes. Its jaws are of equal length and the snout is nearly straight. They have small mouths and a shallow fork in the tail. The colour varies with the water conditions but ranges from almost black through to a light grey on the back, with silver sides and a white belly. They have been known to reach up to 8kg in weight but fish in the 0.5 to 1.5 kg range are more common.

HABITAT

Silver perch prefer faster flowing waters and will occupy areas where the water is slightly more turbulent than that preferred by other native fish in the Murray. They spawn in the spring and summer and will migrate great distances to their spawning grounds. The female will lay in excess of 250,000 eggs. These hatch in a few days and the young perch are able to feed freely on their own. As the silver perch is a schooling fish they are sometimes caught in large numbers.

HOW TO CATCH A SILVER PERCH

BAIT

The best baits for silver perch are shrimp and worms but they have been caught on baits intended for bigger fish and enjoy a good feed of bardi grubs. They are very adept at quickly removing the juiciest bits of the bardi grub, leaving nothing but the skin. The best way to combat this is to either stop fishing with grubs or move to a different location. However if you are specifically targeting silver perch a smaller hook and smaller baits are the go.

LURES

Lure fishing for silver perch is not common practice in the Murray River. However they will attack lures intended for golden perch and can be very aggressive, especially around breeding time. You might like to try some of the smaller plug type lures or the bladed spinner variety.

Occasionally, silver perch will take a lure.

Rod and Reel

A light rod and reel is more suited to the silver perch due to their smaller size. A rod approximately 1.7 metres long with a suitable threadline or baitcaster reel and line to about 3kg breaking strain should set you up nicely to tackle these hard fighting little fish.

Rigs

The most common rigs used to catch silver perch are the Paternoster rig and the running sinker rig with a monofilament (or similar) trace of about 30 centimetres. Hook size is important as the silver perch has a small mouth, but hooks from size 4 down to size 8, depending on the size of the bait, would be most suitable.

Catfish

The catfish is equally at home in salt water as it is in fresh water. Once common and very widespread, they could be found in most inland waterways in Victoria, New South Wales, Queensland and South Australia. However, it is rare to encounter a catfish upstream of Lake Mulwala in the Murray River. This is most likely caused by the cooler water being discharged from large impoundments such as Lake Hume. I personally have not caught a catfish at any point along the Murray River in 40 years of fishing there. This does not mean that there are no catfish there. They are present but they prefer the backwaters and billabongs where they are out of the main flow of the river.

Description

The catfish is rather an odd looking fish. It has a head that you would associate with a "normal fish", the whiskers of a cat but the tail of an eel. It has a down-turned mouth with thick rubbery lips and whiskers or barbels arranged around it. These "whiskers" are used in the catfish's search for food. This fish has no scales and the skin is smooth to the touch.

Caution is needed when handling the cat fish as it has strong serrated spikes on the dorsal and pectoral fins. These spikes are POISONOUS and can inflict a nasty wound.

Habitat

Catfish can be found in the freshwater billabongs and lagoons. They prefer to remain out of the faster flowing water of the river proper. They browse on weed growth and will sift through the mud and silt on the bottom of the slower moving rivers and backwaters. They will move around freely at night and will feed actively during the hours of darkness.

Catfish are slowly disappearing from the Murray-Darling system.

Catfish will usually remain in one area and do not migrate for spawning like the Murray cod or golden perch. The catfish's spawning is not triggered by the spring and summer floods but by the rise in water temperature in these seasons. They will make a nest out of gravel which is usually about .5 to 2.0 metres in diameter. The catfish conduct a courtship ritual above the nest and then the female will release the eggs. The male fertilises the eggs which sink down to the nest. One of the parents will remain on guard duty at the nest until the eggs hatch in around seven days.

How to Catch a Catfish

Bait

Probably the best bait for catfish is worms. They are also very partial to shrimp or a well presented yabbie tail. They have been known to snack on the odd bardi grub too. The catfish uses its down-turned mouth in a vacuum cleaner fashion and will search through the mud for food, so it is wise to fish with baits on the bottom.

Lures

There is little I can tell you about lure fishing for catfish. It is very rare to catch a catfish on lures. However they have been caught on lures and this usually occurs when the lure passes close to the catfish's nest. The parent on guard duty will attack the lure, or for that matter anything that is perceived as a threat to the well being of the eggs.

Rods and Reels

A light spinning rod to about 1.8 metres long with a matching threadline reel would be ideal and this should be married up with 3 to 5 kilogram line. It is wise when fishing at night to incorporate some kind of a device that will assist you in locating or seeing your rod in the dark. Some things that you might like to try are those little bells that you attach to the end of your fishing rod or the mini chemical lights. These items can be purchased from your local tackle dealer.

Rigs

A running sinker rig is probably the best rig to use when fishing for catfish. Use a light ball sinker as it is likely that you will be fishing relatively still or slow moving water. A heavier sinker may also have the effect of restricting the movement of the bait. This would prevent the fish from sucking the bait in freely which in turn could cause the fish to reject your offering. Set your rig up so the sinker is free to run down to the eye of the hook. A fairly small hook, say in the size range 6 to 4, would be ideal. The choice of hook is yours to make but remember that the catfish has thick rubbery lips and so a very sharp hook is advisable.

Murray Crayfish

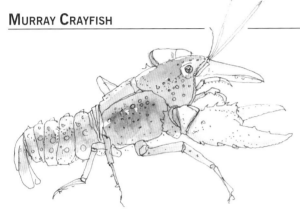

The Murray crayfish is variously known as the "Spiny Freshwater Crayfish", "Freshwater Crayfish" or "Freshwater Lobster". It is the second largest freshwater crayfish in the world and is a much sought after delicacy. A lot of fishermen spend the winter months chasing crayfish. It is found not only in the Murray River, as the name would imply, but also in the Murrumbidgee River and in many of the tributaries of both these rivers. It was once found all along the Murray River as far down as Adelaide but due to many external pressures its range has been cut immensely and it is claimed that it has become extinct down river of Mildura.

Murray crayfish breed once a year. Their breeding season starts towards the end of autumn and the start of winter. The female of the species carries her eggs or berry under her tail for more than five months. Once hatched, the young will stay with their mother for three to four weeks. They will moult twice during this time and will come to resemble a fully grown crayfish before leaving their mother. Crayfish will reach maturity at 6 to 7 years of age.

Catching Crayfish

Murray crayfish feed when the opportunity presents itself. They eat a variety of things and are omnivores, eating anything from rotting leaves to dead fish or other animals.

A hoop or lift net is the only legal way to catch Murray Crays. You can bait your net with any of a number of things. The most common baits are offal such as bullock's liver or sheep heads and fish carcases or chunks. I have found that a carp left to ripen in the winter sun for a few days, makes an ideal bait. Attach the carcass or chunk of fish to a piece of strong cord and suspend this from the top ring of the net so that the cord spans the diameter of the top hoop. This method allows the crayfish to drop clear of the bait and into the net when lifted.

Folklore has it that the best months to catch crayfish are the months without an "R". However, I find that this is not always the case but to give yourself the best chance I suggest you wait until the first weekend in June before venturing out. A couple of good frosts is a good indication that the crayfish are on the move. It would be prudent for you to err on the side of caution when going after crayfish because if you take them too early in the season the meat is not "set" (the flesh is too watery). This means that the tail and claws etc. are not fully formed inside the shell and there would be little meat when cooked.

There are certain regulations governing the use and size of hoop nets in NSW. They are as follows:

- Only five (5) nets per person may be used;
- The diameter of the net is to be no more than 1.25 metres with a drop of not more than 1 metre.
- The mesh size is to be no smaller than 13mm;
- Each net must be clearly tagged with your name and address; The size of the tag must be at least 75mm x 25mm.

There are heavy penalties for any person caught contravening these regulations.

There are many waters that are closed to the taking of crayfish in both New South Wales and Victoria. Be sure to check with the local authorities or tackle dealer before going out. It is also illegal to take female crays in berry. ANY crayfish taken in this condition MUST be returned to the water immediately and with a minimum of fuss. Many people have tried to fool fisheries inspectors by scraping off the berry. This is probably the most common offence committed but this act is easily detected by the trained eye. The bottom line is return any female crayfish with berry to the water.

Murray cray, caught by the author on a Stumpjumper lure!

INTRODUCED SPECIES

There are a number of introduced species in the Murray River. Some of these were introduced intentionally while others were not. The rainbow and brown trout are held in some regard by many fishermen the world over and Australia is no exception. In the Murray though, they are pretty well restricted in their range to the upper reaches of the river. They become less frequent as the waters of the Murray begin to warm up further downstream.

Less glamorous species such as the English perch or redfin and the much maligned European carp are a much more hardy fish and can be found almost all over south eastern Australia. The introduced species will compete with native fish for food and habitat and have caused their own kind of environmental destruction. In many waterways, carp in particular have dirtied the water to such a degree that native fish are unable to tolerate the poor water conditions and have slowly declined in numbers. However there is anecdotal evidence that suggests that in some areas the native fish numbers are on the rise which may also indicate a long overdue downturn in carp populations.

REDFIN

The English perch or redfin is a fast growing fish. It is very aggressive and can be partly blamed for the decline in native fish stock. They are prone to population explosions when there is an abundance of food. This results in massive populations of stunted fish which may not reach any real size. Having said that though, a population of reasonably good sized fish will remain. These may range anywhere from a half to two kilograms in weight.

DESCRIPTION

The redfin could be described as handsome. It is olive to green on the back and sides, has a white belly and five to six black bars on its flanks. These become less obvious in larger fish. The tail and pelvic and anal fins are red to bright orange, hence the name "redfin". It has a large head and mouth. There is a hump behind the head which becomes more pronounced in larger fish. The scales are large and thick and reach well forward on to the gill covers and cheeks. They have been known to grow to immense sizes and the largest recorded redfin caught in Australia weighed in excess

of 10.4 kilograms. A fish this size is extremely rare as redfin usually grow to an average size of one to two kilograms.

HABITAT

Reddies can be found in still and slow flowing waters and like to hide amongst weed beds and other vegetation. You can also find them in overgrown banks and areas of drowned timber. They spawn in spring and the females pass eggs through a temporary pore in their skin. The eggs are very small and are laid in long strings. They are dispersed amongst submerged rocks, vegetation etc. The eggs taste bad to other fish or predators and are therefore protected. The eggs will hatch in a few weeks and the young will form large shoals for a while before they disperse and go their own way.

HOW TO CATCH A REDFIN

BAIT AND LURES

The redfin is a very aggressive feeder and will readily take any of a number of baits and lures. In fact they will eagerly take bait or lures aimed at golden perch. As their mouth is very big they will often take a bait that appears to be far too big for them to handle. The bait used for redfin fishing is almost the same as that used when fishing for other species such as golden perch, namely worms, shrimps and yabbies. As for lures, they will take lures up to about 100mm in length and can be caught using the bladed type of lure such as Celtas or similar.

RODS, REELS AND RIGS

A light spinning rod of about 1.8 metres in length married up with a suitable reel loaded with 3 to 6 kilogram line would suit almost any condition for redfin fishing. Use the Paternoster or running sinker rigs with hooks in the size 4 to size 1 range and you can't go too far wrong.

TECHNIQUES

Once you have located the redfin you can keep them in one area by the use of berley. The pellet type of berley has worked well for me in the past. Breadcrumbs are also another good berley but you will need to give them some weight to get them down and keep them where the fish are.

A moving bait seems to work a little better than a static one. You can impart a bit of movement to your bait by simply lifting the rod tip and lowering it again. This method works particularly well when fishing around drowned trees etc. This "bobbing" technique is deadly when combined with a small heavy jig. A bright chrome colour is best, simply bounce it up and down off the bottom to achieve the desired effect. Very few redfin can resist such an offering.

Drift fishing on large impoundments is also a very effective way to locate and catch the fish. When drift fishing allow your rig to go all the way to the bottom, make a couple of winds of the reel handle to raise it out of the mud and this should get you at just about the right depth. The boat should be allowed to drift with the wind or current until the fish are found. At this point you can drop anchor and get your berley trail going. This should see you catch a good number of reddies. Redfin are arguably one of the best freshwater table fish in the country.

CARP

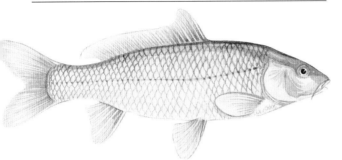

Carp were introduced as early as the 1850s, initially for ornamental purposes and then later in 1961 for aquaculture. They were either liberated accidentally or have escaped from captivity. The various species of carp found the inland waterways of Australia to be very much to their liking. They have bred quickly and are able to survive in conditions that would quickly destroy native fish. They have become a bit of a scapegoat in the debate about the decline of native fish stocks but there is anecdotal evidence to suggest that the native fish in the mid reaches of the Murray may be gaining the upper hand. When ever I go fishing and catch a carp they always seem to be quite large. In fact I can quite honestly say that I have not caught a carp less than a kilogram in weight for over two years. This would seem to suggest that the mortality rate in young carp is very high. While there is no doubt whatsoever that they have contributed to the decline of our natives, they are not entirely to blame. Carp would not be here if it were not for the vanity and carelessness of white Australians.

Renowned for their ability to survive in extremely harsh conditions, carp are found over a vast stretch of Australia's inland waters. They inhabit all of the Murray /Darling system, the Murrumbidgee River and can also be found in all of the impoundments and tributaries to these major rivers. Tasmania was thought to be the only carp free zone in the country, however there are a number of lakes in Tasmania which now boast their own populations of carp. In some states it is illegal to return carp to the water. It is advisable however not to return any carp to the water anywhere at anytime, take them home, feed them to the cat, make fertiliser out of them or turn them into cray baits, but don't return them to the water.

DESCRIPTION

Carp are an elongated fish which has an arched back. The head is medium sized, their eyes and mouths are small and they have thick lips. The mouth can be extended to enable the carp to filter feed on the vegetable matter and other debris on the river or lake bed. Their colouration varies from a pale gold to bronze on the back and their scales have a dark edging which gives them a "meshed" appearance. They have a couple of fleshy barbels at the corner of their mouths and their fins have a reddish tint. The anal and leading edge of the dorsal fin have very sharp serrated spines on them which are capable of causing a nasty wound. The design of these spines can be likened to that of the barb on a fish hook. It goes in easily but is very difficult to remove.

HABITAT

Carp can tolerate extreme water conditions and low oxygen levels and can generally be found in still or slowly moving waters. Carp particularly like areas that offer a generous growth of aquatic vegetation.

Their breeding is dictated by water temperatures and they usually start their spawning in the spring when the water temperature starts to rise. A female carp weighing around 6 kilograms can lay up to 1.5 million eggs. That is a phenomenal amount and you can easily see how they have come to almost overrun some waterways. The young carp grow very quickly in shallow warm water where there is plenty of food. They can attain lengths of 70 centimetres in 2 years.

HOW TO CATCH A CARP

BAIT AND LURES

Carp are very opportunistic feeders and will take just about any bait you offer them. They will eat bottom vegetation, crustaceans, other aquatic creatures and particularly like worms. In fact all the conventional freshwater baits are effective on carp. I have heard of folks who have caught carp on tomatoes and others who have used pieces of cheese. Corn kernels are another great alternative.

Lures are not often used when fishing for carp but they will sometimes attack lures with gusto. This is a rare occurrence and they will usually only attack a lure when forced to protect their domain.

RODS, REELS AND RIGS

Using light gear on carp is always fun as they can grow to quite a size and are very strong swimmers. They have a tail that resembles a shovel blade and this gives them a good purchase on the water. A rod in excess of 1.8 metres coupled with a reel loaded with 4-5 kilogram line should see you have a bit of fun. Keep your rig very basic. A small sinker and fairly small hook, about size 4 to 6 will be sufficient. Coarse angling methods are becoming increasingly popular when fishing for carp.

COLLECTING BAIT

There are many different types of bait that can be used to catch freshwater fish. Strangely enough though, not all baits used for freshwater fish come from fresh water. In fact some of the things that are used for bait don't come from the water at all, for example salt water mussels, prawns, bardi grubs, earth worms and so on. I often wonder how fish know that it is food in front of them when that particular item is alien to their environment. I have already mentioned the baits that will catch various fish, and will concentrate here on how you can obtain the bait that is used to catch cod and other fish in the Murray River.

BARDI GRUBS

Grubs are arguably the best bait for cod. Many different species of grubs can be used but without doubt the best and most commonly used is the bardi grub. They are the larval form of the goat moth. Quite large, and creamy white in colour, they can be found under red gum trees.

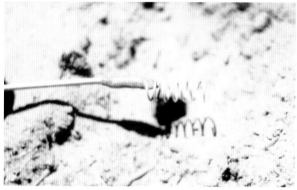

ABOVE: A bardi grub wire and hole. The bardi grub wire is made from speedometer cable with spring attached.

BELOW: Extracting bardi grubs from holes using a bardi grub wire.

You can obtain a supply of bardi grubs in a couple of ways. Buying them from a local supplier can be very expensive as a single bardi grub can cost anywhere from $1.50 to two dollars. A day's fishing can be become very expensive proposition especially when your bait is continuously pinched by small fish and carp.

Alternatively you can gather your own. The first step in gathering your own supply of grubs is to kit yourself out with a few necessities. Arm yourself with a good sharp bladed shovel, a garden rake and a long flexible wire. The long flexible wire is used for extracting the grub from it's hole. It can be made from just about anything but it is most commonly made from a disused speedo cable with a different sized spring attached to each end, this cable needs to be a minimum of 1.2metres long. Alternatively you can buy a ready made grub wire from a tackle store.

To reach your grub, chip away the top couple of inches of leaf matter and soil from your selected spot. This should uncover the grubs hole. If you don't find the hole in the first few inches of soil you may need to dig down, maybe up to 30 to 40 centimetres. You should avoid damaging the root system of the tree in your search. If you come across the tree roots try searching along the length of the root as bardi grubs can sometimes be found there. Once you have found the hole insert the flexible wire into the hole and slide it down until you feel the grub at the end. Now twist the wire a quarter of a turn and withdraw the wire (and grub) in one smooth action. Only give the wire a quarter of a turn as this will gently pierce the grub's skin and won't damage or tear the grub.

Bardi grubs will stay alive for some time after capture. The longevity of your grubs depends entirely on the way you store them. First and foremost, it is very important to store them separately as they will attack and kill each other. Once I get my collection of grubs home I wash them clean of dirt and other debris. I check them all to see if they are dead or alive and separate the damaged from the undamaged ones. The live grubs are stored individually in cigarette packets or a compartmentalised box. Once this is done they are placed in a cool spot. The bottom of the fridge is a good place (ask your wife first!) or try a very cool spot in your home. Those grubs that haven't survived or are damaged can be stored indefinitely in the freezer. They also need to be prepared for storage. This is done by blanching them for about 30 seconds in boiling water or milk. Once they are blanched dry them off and place them in a container. It is important that you dry them otherwise when the time comes to use them they will be frozen together in a lump. A less common way of storing the grub is to pickle them in brine. These also need to be kept cool. Ideally place them in a jar and stick them in the fridge. Obviously fresh live grubs are the best bait for cod but your frozen or pickled ones will do just fine too.

YABBIES

Yabbies are an excellent bait for a variety of freshwater fish. Obviously they vary greatly in size but generally resemble a miniature lobster. The colours vary depending on the environment and range from a light brown through to black. Yabbies can be used for more than just bait and are often caught as a delicacy for the table. They are delicious, and an export market for them has been opened by some enterprising individuals. Yabbie farms have been established to cater for the food and export market.

You can buy yabbies for bait but it is much more enjoyable to catch your own. There are a variety of yabbie nets commercially available. Drop nets and opera house nets are a couple of examples. Most of the nets are ideally suited to waters that have a fairly clean bottom. Enclosed nets such as the opera house net have a "sock" in them which is provided for you to put the bait in and will stop the yabbies from making a complete mess of it. The enclosed nets can, once set, be left in position for quite some time before they need to be checked, even overnight isn't out of the question.

Drop nets are a different proposition as the bait is tied into the bottom of the net using a bit of cord. These nets need to be checked on a very regular basis as the yabbies can enter and leave the net at will. You should raise your drop net in a smooth lifting motion to prevent the yabbies from escaping.

The last type of net we will talk about is the scoop net. As with other nets, there are number of styles going around. You can buy good quality scoop nets from your local tackle store or you can fashion one yourself from any suitable materials. To catch yabbies using a scoop net, simply extend the net to its full length into the water and drag it back along the bottom through the weed beds and such. Do this two or three times before you empty the net. Once you have taken what you need you should sort the yabbies into sizes. You need to do this as the larger yabbies will attack and kill the smaller ones.

Nets are not the only thing you can use to catch yabbies. Another way, which is probably more fun than using a net, is to use a piece of cord or even cotton

John Knight lifting a yabby drop pot baited with European carp. Great for catching your fishing bait or just a day out with the kids.

with your bait tied to the end. For bait you should use a piece of raw meat, but in a pinch cooked meat will work. You only need to use a fairly short piece of string, just drop it in the water at the edge of the channel or dam. Give yourself a little bit of slack and wait, when you notice the slack being taken up, slowly draw the string upwards. Slide your net underneath and catch your yabbie. Please remember to only take what you need and return the rest to the water.

Yabbies will stay alive indefinitely after capture with very little maintenance. Ideally you would place them in a container such as a baby bath or small plastic kiddies pool or similar. Put a few inches of water in it and a few stones for cover. I like to use the bricks with holes in them as these give the yabbies somewhere to hide. Place them in a shady spot in a quiet part of the garden. Feed them with grated carrot. Don't feed them meat as this will go off and foul the water. Speaking of water, don't forget to change the water every week or so or when the water becomes discoloured. You must also remember to remove any dead yabbies daily.

When going fishing, only take enough yabbies for the trip. You can put them in a small foam container such as a "six pack" Esky with a couple of inches of water in it. Remember to change this water every few hours on warm days. If you are going away for an extended period put your yabbies in a larger foam container covered with a couple of inches of water and

Yabbies like these are a treat to eat and are readily available in the Barmah Lakes after a good flood.

a dampened sugar bag, potato sack or a clean piece of hessian type fabric. This will stop the water splashing and keep your yabbies cool. Another good way to keep your yabbies alive is to construct a net or bag from a piece of shade cloth material. This can be left in a shady part of the river.

When collecting yabbies from farm dams or private property make sure you get the owners permission before entering. Be sure to check the regulations governing the type and use of nets in your area as they vary from state to state. The use of Opera house nets is banned in Victoria.

Shrimp

Freshwater shrimp are a very good bait for a large number of fish but they are generally not available from bait retailers. You can gather shrimp at your fishing location using a net or a shrimp tin. Nets are obtainable from a tackle or disposal store, and are constructed from a light netting material surrounding a spring wire frame. Shrimp nets incorporate a couple of zippers and an interior pocket. The smaller zip give you access to the pocket, whilst the larger of the zips gives you a quick and easy way of getting any shrimp out of the net with a minimum of fuss. Collapsible for easy and convenient storage the nets are probably the easiest way to catch shrimp.

Nets can be baited with a piece of unscented soap or another very effective bait, the carcass of your last roast chicken and add a sprig of fresh gum leaves to provide cover. Place your net in a spot where there are some reeds, tree roots, weed beds or some other shelter that is out of the glare of the sun. Try putting it in a spot that is away from the current as this can cause your net to become tangled which may also keep it off the bottom.

If your budget doesn't run to a manufactured shrimp net, try making a shrimp trap of your own. To do this you will need a large tin, such as a large coffee tin, a 4 litre paint tin or even a 20 litre drum. Make sure that you thoroughly clean out any tin you use. In the sides of the tin make a series of slits and on the bottom a series of holes. The slits and holes need to big enough to allow the water to drain quickly but not too big to allow the shrimp escape when retrieving your trap. To complete your work tie a piece of strong cord to the top or handle. The cord needs to be long enough to enable you get the trap in to the right place and leave enough to secure it to the bank or snag. Throw a good size sprig of gum leaves in the tin to cover your bait as this will trick the shrimp into thinking they have plenty of cover and stop them from bolting when you drag your trap out of the water. Set it in the same manner as your net ensuring that it lies on its side to give the shrimp easy access.

As with all baits, shrimp are best used alive, however they will die quickly when taken from the water. But with a little care you can keep your shrimp in good condition for the duration of your trip. You can achieve this by leaving your shrimp net in the water and only taking out what you need for immediate use, or if you are in a boat, put them in a container that can be thrown over the side and allows the water to flow through it. Another good alternative is a battery powered aerator.

BELOW: Nat Tyler with two different shrimp net tins.

LEFT: Shrimp can also be collected in drop pots. Freeze them between pieces of wet kitchen paper to keep fresh for fishing.

Dead shrimp are a reasonable bait too, they are also a bit easier to store. You can place them in the deep freeze, in a container of damp saw dust or between layers of damp paper towel. In this way the shrimp will maintain their natural colour and can be kept indefinitely. There are regulations covering the use of shrimp traps so check with the relevant state authorities which are listed on page seven before you start.

WORMS

Worms. What can I say? They have to be the most common bait ever used. Almost anyone who has ever fished has probably used worms as bait. Worms come in a few different types and are widely available. The big scrub worms are by far the best bait and the African night crawlers would be a close second. Garden worms are an effective reserve but can be hard to come by when the weather is very hot and dry.

Worms can be kept alive indefinitely with a bit of attention and care. A large foam or polystyrene container, such as the type used by fruiterers, is ideal. Half fill this with a light mixture of damp soil, manure or some other organic material and put the worms into it. Cover this with damp paper or hessian and put the box in a cool, shady spot.

Worms can be fed with vegetable peelings, just throw them in the box to keep the worms satisfied. If you want to keep a large colony of worms just use bigger containers to keep them in. But it should be noted that in order to keep them healthy and strong you may need to divide the volume of worms in each container every couple of months.

Presentation of the worm when fishing is very important. Thread the worm onto the hook so it is covered, leaving nice wriggly bits on each end. If your worms are fairly small put enough on to cover the hook. Of course this has the added benefit of giving you more wriggling ends. I would recommend that you always take a punnet of worms on your fishing trips as they are a great stand-by bait. And don't forget to keep them cool and out of the sun or else they will quickly die.

African night crawlers are excellent worms for attracting fish, but they die easily if not kept cool.

OTHER THINGS FISH EAT

There are many amazing stories recounting the gastronomical feats of cod. There are stories of Murray cod taking birds drinking at the water's edge and their stomachs contents including ducks, rabbits, whole freshwater spiny crayfish and recently, golf balls. Obviously using birds, rabbits and golf balls as bait should not even be considered but when you think about it, there are a great number of other things you can try such as sweet corn kernels, pieces of red meat, hard boiled eggs or fresh water mussels.

There are things you cannot use as bait and among these are frogs, finned fish, baby birds and other protected animals. Not only is the use of such things against the law, it is barbaric and cruel. The bottom line is, if you think it will work give it a try, you have nothing to lose!

FISH FOR THE TABLE

It is often said that the most expensive fish you eat is the one you catch yourself. This is probably true when you consider the amount of time and effort spent on catching and preparing your fish. If this isn't done the right way, all your time and effort may amount to nothing.

Part of the fun of fishing is taking a fish for the table. To get the best out of the fish it is important that you prepare it in the right way. All too often people treat their catch incorrectly, and as a result the eating quality of the fish is spoiled.

On capture the fish should be despatched as soon and as possible. This is done by inflicting a strong blow to the head or by cutting the throat. The fish should be cleaned, filleted and put on ice as soon as you can manage it. The longer you leave this the more likely it is that bacteria and other gremlins will have a chance to start breeding. Alternatively you can keep the fish alive in a keeper net which can be left in the water or in a suitably sized container of water. If you are going to use a container you may need to change the water occasionally or you can aerate the water using a portable battery powered aerator.

If killing the fish straight away ensure that you "bleed" the fish, remove the guts and gills and put the fish on ice. Ice slurry or crushed ice is the most suitable for this purpose.

The next stage of the preparation comes when you get home. It's now time for you to either cook and eat the fish or prepare it for long term storage. The size of the fish will give you an indication on a suitable method of cooking. Smaller fish can be cooked whole or filleted while the larger fish can be filleted or cut into collars.

If you are going to freeze the fish or fish pieces it is a good idea to batch them into convenient meal sized parcels. After you cut the fish up make sure that you dry the pieces with a piece of paper towel or tea towel. If you don't do this the excess liquid can cause the flesh to become soft when thawed out. A couple of other things you should consider is to seal the flesh in air tight bags and to mark the bags with the date. Remember, it is advisable not to keep fish in the freezer for more than 3 months.

COOKING THE CATCH

Once the fish is prepared for the pot all that remains is for you or someone else (who can cook) to cook it. Obviously there is more than one way to do this. Although I rarely kill fish these days, I am still partial to a feed of fresh fish. What I will pass on to you now are some of my favourite recipes.

BAKED FISH

- **Fish (fillets or whole)** • **Lemon slices**
- **Knobs of butter**   • **Chopped Parsley**
- **Salt and Pepper**

Place the fish on a piece of tin foil. Arrange the other ingredients over the fish and fold the tin foil into a pouch. Place this in a moderate oven for about 20 to 30 minutes. The time might vary depending on the thickness of the fillets. If you are cooking a whole fish you can stuff the body cavity with the ingredients.

BATTERED FISH

- **Fillets of your favourite fish** • **Eggs**
- **Self raising flour**   • **Olive Oil**
- **Beer, water or milk**

Mix your egg and flour together and add the liquid (your choice). Mix until all the ingredients are well blended. Dip your fish into the batter mix. If the batter runs off it's too thin, add more flour. Then place the coated fillets into a pan of hot olive oil and cook for about ten minutes. Turn the fillets until they are golden brown on both sides.

COOKING MURRAY CRAYFISH

A pot large enough to fit your crayfish is needed. Half fill the pot with water and bring it to the boil. Once the water is boiling add a little salt and a sprinkle of vinegar. Alternatively you can add a slice of lemon. While the water is boiling add your crayfish and bring the water back to boil. Allow this to boil for 15 to 20 minutes then take it out and put it into another pot filled with cold water. Leave it in the cold water until it is cool. When cool remove it from the water and allow it to drain. Clean and prepare a dressing made from vinegar, salt and pepper; alternatively you can mix the meat with mayonnaise.

Another way to eat crayfish tails is to place them in a frypan with a small amount of butter and heat until hot. Turn off the heat at this point and add a dessert spoon of honey and sprinkle sesame seeds over the lot and stir until the meat is coated with the honey and seeds.

Outlaw
Australia's Most WANTED Spinnerbaits

Australian made quality.
Weights range from 1/8th oz to a massive 3 oz troller
80 colours to choose from.

Tougher than the rest, so use the best!

Fish with confidence around the snags!

www.outlawspinnerbaits.com.au